D0491910

YOU MAY WELL ASK

BY THE SAME AUTHOR:

WHEN THE BOUGH BREAKS

THE CORN KING AND THE SPRING QUEEN

THE BLOOD OF THE MARTYRS

THE BIG HOUSE

TRAVEL LIGHT

TO THE CHAPEL PERILOUS

MEMOIRS OF A SPACEWOMAN

SOLUTION THREE

THE CLEANSING OF THE KNIFE
(poems)

IMAGES OF AFRICA

Autobiography

SMALL TALK...:
Memoirs of an Edwardian Childhood

ALL CHANGE HERE:
Girlhood and Marriage

Naomi Mitchison in the 1920s

Naomi Mitchison

YOU MAY WELL ASK

A Memoir 1920–1940

LONDON
VICTOR GOLLANCZ LTD
1979

First impression July 1979
Second impression September 1979

ISBN 0 575 02614 6

PRINTED IN GREAT BRITAIN
BY EBENEZER BAYLIS AND SON LTD
THE TRINITY PRESS, WORCESTER, AND LONDON

CONTENTS

LIST OF ILLUSTRATIONS

ACKNOWLEDGEMENTS

The author is grateful to the following for permission to quote from letters included in Part II: the University of Manchester for letters of Professor Alexander; Mrs Laura Huxley for letters of Aldous Huxley; the Society of Authors on behalf of the Provost and Scholars of King's College, Cambridge, for letters of E. M. Forster; Jay Michael Barrie for letters from Gerald Heard; Edward Mendelson for letters from W. H. Auden; Mrs Agnes Stapledon for letters from Olaf Stapledon; the Society of Authors and Mrs G. A. Wyndham Lewis for letters from Wyndham Lewis; James MacGibbon for letters from Stevie Smith.

ACKNOWLEDGMENTS

[illegible]

SETTING THE SCENE

IT WAS THE end of 1918 and the First World War was over and everything which had happened before was going to come back. Or was it? No. Some had survived. My brother in the Black Watch, J. B. S. Haldane, was one of them, partly no doubt because he had been wounded twice and out of it for at least several months. But the others, our friends, our lives and happiness together? No.

Dick, my husband, by then a major, had got himself demobbed quickly. He had passed his Bar exams during sick leave when he was supposed to be resting his brain after the fractured skull which had got him out of the front line for months, to be followed by a staff course and then a year and a half as liaison officer between the British and French armies in Italy. He longed to get back to real life—'civvy street'—and make a new start.

But first of all where were we going to live? My mother and my mother-in-law who tended to disagree about most things were firmly agreed about the necessity for a house. In December 1918 I thought and perhaps even said how nice it would be to live in a flat. It seemed so modern! Dick and Bey Gillespie had shared a flat in Wynnstay Gardens behind Barkers. Why not me? But my dear, they said, the baby, the nurse, the cook! So house agents were consulted and 17 Cheyne Walk was bought. Chelsea was not such a good neighbourhood as Kensington or Westminster but very suitable for young people. And here we lived from early 1919 until 1923.

Before we moved in we had been going over every evening to my parents-in-law. Dick's younger brother Willie had rushed into the war in 1914 as a despatch rider and been wounded twice but unhappily not severely enough to keep him out of it; after his death in action Dick's parents had moved from their very large house on Chelsea Embankment to a smaller but still large house in Eaton Place, and for some time kept on their Surrey country house, Frolbury, as well. The London house was overheated; Dick played bridge with his parents and I settled down gloomily with a book; I had never learnt to play cards, which always seemed to me too like hard work, as well as being in an unbelieved-in but convenient sense the devil's pictures.

We were so anxious to get into our own house that we moved into Cheyne Walk and slept there in a big oak double bed we had bought in Burford, though the sheets and blankets had not yet come. I bought prepared cutlets in the King's Road and cooked them on a gas stove whose workings still alarmed me. You wouldn't think one could spoil cutlets. I did.

But who was I? I was now twenty-one, married in 1916 to a young husband on short leave and now with a young baby, but scarcely adult in any real sense. Who and why I was is set out in two earlier books, *Small Talk* and *All Change Here*. This book will try to show honestly how I grew up and changed into the woman I was when the next war came. But it will be about a family and the friends and acquaintances, fellow workers and fellow voters who shaped us as we in turn shaped them.

In this book I shall inevitably refer to public events and people well known at the time but unfamiliar to some of today's readers, for whom all this is 'history' and because of that rather a bore and unimportant compared with their real lives and the immediate events which are shaping them. It would take another book to stop and explain everything. I have to press on. It was my life. It has been hard to write. The nearer it comes to the present the more difficult it is to write honestly about the past. One is still involved. Bits of it are still powerful to hurt or to recall stupidities and bad judgement and cruelties, perhaps inadvertent or perhaps not.

If it is all to have any value the writer must be honest about what is actually remembered. It would be dishonest to consult history or gossip books written by other people about a great event in which as a matter of fact the writer didn't take part and which she remembers only vaguely and from the sheltered edge. However, there is plenty of other evidence which I have kept on consulting: now and then I kept diaries. In the late Thirties, when I was on the Mass Observation national panel, I produced some evidence once a month, as we all did, and I kept a 'war diary' with considerable detail. There are letters which I can use both to jog my memory and set the trains of pictures going and also because they date events and often show what I was actually doing at a given time. My own books are important for all this, especially those which have pencilled notes about where and when they were written, and sometimes about the people or places which were to some extent acting as models.

During all these years I used small pocket diaries which give a bit of sketchy information. They list things that had to be remembered: children's dentist appointments, school holiday breaks, committee meetings and dinner parties, but seldom the major events of our life. They usually have lists of books I intended to read or sometimes to buy. They may well have lists of things I wanted, usually a Christmas present list and some accounts. But some of them have great gaps where perhaps I lost the diary temporarily as one always does. A few have fairly accurate botanical drawings of flowers with notes which I could probably use for identifying them; this was usually when I had been abroad, and my copy of Bentham and Hooker in which I ticked off the plants I found has dates and places for these. Apart from this I have a book with notes of the guests at dinner parties, and occasional comments. For that matter some of my old dresses are still there in the acting box.

Besides all that, in the diaries themselves and sometimes in other books I used to put down quotations, usually from poems, which give my state of mind. But perhaps 'mind' is the wrong word. 'Emotional state' would be more accurate. I also wrote poems in the diaries, I am sure in all of them, every single one. Some of these are reasonably good and found their way first on to the typewriter, later perhaps into books. Others are expressions of immediate emotions (usually) or else the way some landscape or town struck me. Yet poetry ought to be the most economical and hard-hitting way of expressing feelings which lose so much of their force in the niggling accuracies and qualifications of prose.

There is thus plenty of evidence on which to base this book. But take care! Memory can be remarkably inaccurate. Without intending to we cancel and invent or imagine. This happens worst in periods where we are likely to be in a state of emotional stress or disorder, which is fairly usual for a great many people, especially those in the arts. Or again if we are actively engaged in something we tend to remember our successes and to rub out the failures and shames. Clearly I am no better than the rest.

And so back to our start as a respectable married couple. At the beginning of 1919 we knew very few people of our own age in London. My parents-in-law, still devastated by the death of their younger son, could not help us much. We looked for something of the old cheerful life of pre-war adolescence. It had gone for ever. I was pregnant again on purpose but with some discomfort.

I went to Oxford for the birth of the next two children, Denny in 1919, Murdoch in 1922. I still hadn't cut the strings between myself and the Oxford ambience of my girlhood life in my parents' house which I wrote about in *All Change Here*. I still in a way felt myself more child than mother. Up till 1925 my brother was still there, either at New College or at home; he and Dick and I together enjoyed ourselves almost as much as before the war, and some of the others came back for a year or two: Gervas and Aldous Huxley, Lewis Gielgud. My mother took charge of the babies. Lazily I accepted this and afterwards when I wanted to pull out of it found it difficult to do so. I still loved dancing, and when we went to Oxford I still canoed and punted and swam in the Cherwell in a slightly less enveloping bathing dress than my pre-war blue serge which had covered my knees and elbows.

So this was the beginning of our married life and the bringing up of a family. It was the beginning for Dick of the struggle at the Bar and political interests gradually emerging. For me it was attempting to be a competent wife and mother according to the ideas of the time, but above all it was the intense inward excitement out of which I wrote my first book, *The Conquered.*

I

Patterns of Living

THE CLASS STRUCTURE AS IT SEEMED TO US

BEFORE WORLD WAR I and with a hangover into the Twenties at least, middle- or professional-class housing depended on having servants to cook, clean and generally take charge. Most houses, especially the older ones, had this as their norm. Now this pattern of having servants is probably the strangest part of our lives for those two generations on who may well find the idea not only embarrassing but definitely shocking. Too bad. For us, in what I suppose I should call the upper middle class, having servants was part of the normal pattern of life. We took it for granted.

For me the servant basis meant that I could have parties, without having to think about the washing up, in the ground-floor dining room and the very pretty L-shaped drawing room on the first floor of 17 Cheyne Walk, with its two tall windows looking out on to a balcony, high shelves at the back of the L, a sofa, an Italian table we had picked up at a country auction, and comfortable armchairs from Dick's old flat so well made that they are still with us. There was an electric fire but I doubt if we were yet used to today's standards of indoor warmth.

Above this was our bedroom with a lovely view across the trees and the river, off it a dressing room usually serving as a child's room, and a bathroom. On the floor above was the nursery at the front with an even better view. Behind it a double and crowded maids' room. I am sure another bathroom was squeezed in but after a couple of years we added a storey, sloping back with dormers, for by then we had two children and another on the way, as well as cook, housemaid, parlour maid and nurse. It wasn't expensive to have an addition like this put on to a house and I don't believe we gave it very much thought.

A crazily overgrown home for a young professional-class family? It didn't seem so to us. Other people whom we knew had the same kind of house, though in Oxford there was always a good garden as well. When we went to stay with our Danish friends, the Carstensens, in Copenhagen, they had a flat on Grueningen with the same spaciousness and room for furniture and pictures and also maids. Dick's old army friends whom we visited in Paris seemed more cramped but clearly they preferred to spend their money on good food rather than spacious housing.

In front of our house there was a small paved garden and a covered walk to the front door where one could leave a pram. At the back was a narrow garden between rather high brick walls, well laid out by our predecessors with little stone steps and paving and a tiny lawn at the end. The first thing I did was to plant a mulberry which was just coming into bearing when we left. I never managed to keep the garden quite as nicely as had been done earlier, though I plunged into the delight of buying bedding plants—not very expensive but my mother would have thought this wasteful if not actually immoral.

Of course there was the usual basement with kitchen, scullery, coal cellar and larder. It looked out on to an 'area' scooped out of the little front garden which I tried to enlarge and brighten a little. Here lived Mrs Bell whose cooking was not particularly good and who frightened me. I went down one day to discuss domestic affairs and found her leaning against the table apparently ill, unable to speak properly. I was dreadfully worried, thinking I must get the doctor, when my Scottish housemaid, found for me by Aunt Bay (Elizabeth Haldane), drew me aside and explained that she was drunk and indeed often was. Oh, dear, this was a new one! I ran away leaving it to Dick.

Even after Mrs Bell had been replaced I lived in a state of fear, hoping that my morning interview with the cook would not take too long and that I would not have to 'do the books'. Dick never kept me short of money but I really never knew how much I ought to spend on what. This seems odd now but I had been brought up to consider money as something men dealt with, a bit dirty at that. We simply had a certain standard and I never committed wild extravagances. Anything expensive for the house was always sensibly talked over, but we both bought books, hard-backs of course, whenever we liked. Dick's parents were well off.

His father went on going to the City every day almost until his death; he would have been terribly bored otherwise. They always had a Daimler and chauffeur; Dick's mother had good furs and some beautiful jewellery, and a collection of Dresden and Meissen china. Dick inherited family shares and working directorates as well as his Bar work which for a long time brought in very little. My feeling now is that in the Twenties people could get by quite comfortably on £600–£700 a year, but once there was a family or some kind of 'establishment' most of our friends were into four figures, though not perhaps much more. But most expected to do better year by year, especially in the professions.

Servants' wages went up slowly in all jobs, and were static during the depression of the Thirties. A cook could earn about £1 a week; an upper house- or parlourmaid would have approached this; dresses and aprons were 'found'. All prices were in line with this; a penny was some use to a child. A half-sovereign tip was something really good.

By 1923 we wanted to move to a larger house but not one which would put us into a different social circle. The jump to a really bigger house took one into high society which we rather despised. Hampstead would have been all right but not Golders Green; St John's Wood and Campden Hill were both acceptable though rather arty neighbourhoods. When we moved from Chelsea my in-laws, who had by then given up Frolbury, themselves moved to a really beautiful house somewhere in the centre of Campden Hill with a big garden; I have never managed to find it again. There were other houses in Chelsea but none of the ones we really liked were for sale. When we moved to Hammersmith we found neighbours with similar tastes and standards all along the river right up to Chiswick and round St Peter's Square; many were more or less in the arts, writers, painters and sculptors. There were plenty of children.

River Court, now part of Latimer School, had much bigger rooms than our old house so that we could and did have bigger and better parties. As the years went on we altered and enlarged it, mainly to give better servant accommodation; in the end they had the kind of flat which many a young couple might envy. Originally one of the big basement rooms had been used as a bedroom for a young kitchen maid and under housemaid. One weekend when we were in the country there was a sudden Thames flood over the low river wall. The girls were not trapped, for the water only came halfway up the wall, but being heavy sleepers they simply and shockingly drowned in their beds. After that the river wall was raised.

One of the big basement rooms was used as a kind of laboratory and workroom for the boys as they grew up. There was a large wine cellar and under the garden a disused ice house. It is all described in the *Survey of London*, for indeed it was an historic house built on the site of the Queen Dowager's house and its proportions were good eighteenth century, especially the main staircase with its beautiful sweep upwards. Photographs of the time show the heavy growth of Virginia creeper which we were always cutting back. Later the boys climbed from window to window holding on to it; I begged them not to do it while I was looking.

On the ground floor there was a dining room which could easily take fourteen at table, and a big double drawing room, one end looking into the garden, the other out over the river, while the side window caught the early sun. The walls were painted to look like a very fancy yellow marble; this sounds awful but was a complete success. The furniture looked well against it, and the back room had one wall completely filled with a bookcase and corner cupboards in satinwood, beautifully finished. My desk was in the sunny end. There was a piano and plenty of space. The big T'ang horse stood on the mantelpiece and I at least didn't mind at all that he had clearly been much mended and renovated. Behind the staircase was a study for Dick with high bookcases and a huge Chinese landscape, dark and intricate. The drawing room had an open fire; the marble mantelpieces were lovely and of course we had our books in every room.

Above were the children's rooms, a splendid day nursery, again with an open fire behind an efficient guard, and Vitaglass which was supposed to let in all the good of the sunshine. The boys' room had Chinese wallpaper from Sandersons; in one place it was torn and I painted in a guinea pig and a snail. Above there were more bedrooms, including my own which had a wide *trompe l'œil* cupboard by a young painter, yellow pillars, a dressing table from the Omega Workshops and a splendid view, again over the Thames. There were two large bathrooms, fixed basins (something fairly new at the time) in four of the bedrooms, and two small bedrooms up the back stairs which were less beautiful but quite adequate. Peter the rabbit would hop up and down those stairs, balefully waiting for a cat or dog he could frighten. Above was the flat roof with a stone balustrade, splendid for Boat Race parties. Some time in the Thirties we had a little wooden lean-to built on it behind the main chimney stack and we slept out in summer.

At the end of the garden we added a squash court, designed by John Macgregor with a wavy pattern of bricks and a loggia with concrete pillars and plant boxes blocked into patterns. It has still two bronzes by Gertrude Hermes, the sea horse on the top and a snail fountain. Behind the loggia was my workroom, the only time in my life I've ever had a room simply to write in, a room of my own. John designed a pattern of floor tiles and lots of drawers which I never entirely finished filling up because—well, it made a good air-raid shelter, under the solid floor of the squash court.

The garden had an outer brick wall on Rivercourt Road, on which in the Thirties I used to chalk slogans largely for the pleasure of telling the police who came to reprimand me that the wall was my property and I could do what I chose with it. The front corner of the embankment and Rivercourt Road had an old elm in it, now cut down, which shaded it almost too much and whose roots stopped anything else from growing. In any case I was an ignorant and inefficient gardener. In front of the main house was a smaller garden of which I paved part, heaving unexpectedly heavy bits of crazy paving into place and imagining the crevices filled with thyme and aubrietia rather than the couch grass and dandelions which always took over. I had cut down the enclosing dark privet hedge and now I filled the two narrow beds up to the front door with spring bulbs, crocuses, hyacinths and tulips at a shilling a dozen. The first year they were raided, so I wrote up an elaborate notice saying they were there for everyone's pleasure so please don't pick them. It had the desired effect; there is something interestingly compulsive about a long notice. I probably drew decorations on it too!

In the big garden at the back, which was somewhat of a wilderness when we came, I cut back some things but kept the large bushes of mock orange and handsome plumy spiraea. There was a huge dark yew tree by the back wall but ordinary irises flourished under it and so rather surprisingly did hollyhocks which seeded themselves year after year and produced some really magnificent colours. I planted a double row of espaliered apple trees which blossomed beautifully but seldom yielded much in the way of fruit. They were excellent for hide-and-seek all the same. I also contrived two small ponds, one very shallow, but nowadays I wouldn't have done it since small children will drown in only inches of water. As it was they gave great pleasure.

There were one or two stone sinks with stonecrop, saxifrage and such, and on the trellis between garden and garage a vine which I hadn't learned to prune properly. Peonies grew well except for the year when small Valentine came to me with a handful of lovely green ballies that she had picked off them.

It was a garden for eating out in and for parties. One Midsummer Eve party we had a bonfire and various people jumped over it, one hopes with good results. Clough Williams-Ellis even jumped the garden fence above the brick wall and sprained his ankle. We always had fireworks on 5 November and no child ever got hurt but at one I had a wretched miscarriage. The local children came in and out; it was a good play place, much freer and friendlier than Chelsea. When one of the elms at the end of the road in the bay facing the river finally died I asked if I could plant another tree and after some hesitation the Hammersmith Borough Council agreed. My acacia sapling is a big tree now.

River Court was the kind of house we wanted and I suppose felt we deserved. Our income was such that we could afford the staff which it had to have for its upkeep. But the Upstairs Downstairs relationship was already changing, perhaps everywhere but with us largely because of that nice man Levinson. He had been a ranker captain and came to Dick in the early 1920s as a fellow officer to ask for a job for a few months until he could buy a chicken farm. Dick of course said yes, and this meant a breaking of the old master–servant relationship. The chicken farm never materialised, mostly because of Lev's wife, who was in theory the cook and in practice an alcoholic, dreaming of better things than getting on with the job. Lev himself, though infinitely trustworthy and always much interested in the conversation of the better-known guests when he was pouring the wine at dinner (or once by some inadvertence methylated spirits), was not averse to a spot himself. But he was always charming with the children. He had a nice small boy of his own. We managed to shift Mrs Levinson out of being cook after the first few years; her preferences in cooking always seemed to thwart my own. But Lev was a bit of a flirt and she would intervene noisily and disastrously in someone else's cooking.

Although my time as a VAD nurse at St Thomas's polishing lockers and sweeping floors had taught me a bit about housework, I had, as I have indicated, shamefully little idea about cookery. This, combined with an obscure feeling that good eating was a sinful luxury, ought to have stopped anyone from marrying me. Luckily it had not, and I did some learning though most of it very late. However, for me as for other middle-class wives, married life meant having a cook, who had first to be interviewed, then engaged, though this could be done in a cubicle at a registry office. There were a number of these privately run offices for domestic employment, each having a different speciality—nannies, cooks, butlers and so on—and the staff there helped one and perhaps took up references.

To understand what the household staff did in a house like River Court one has to go back to a period with few disposables; babies' nappies were only just coming in late in the Thirties, though disposable sanitary towels were by then not universal but usual. No fridge, no dishwasher, no electric liquidiser or whisk (instead a hair sieve and rubbing in the fat by hand), no detergents and no drip-dry, for that matter no washing machines or spin-dryers, instead scrubbing with bars of yellow soap and the irons heating on the stove. Sheets and towels went to the laundry, but other things were washed at home; Lux Flakes started in the Thirties, and by then we had an electric iron. Nurse and nursery-maid—Belle was the last—did the children's things, which became more practical after the Twenties with fewer ribbons to be threaded in. Margaret Carey who did my washing was a Scot, steady and kind, an ironer-out of domestic frictions. We used to dry the household washing at River Court on the flat top of the house behind the stone balustrade. Crêpe de Chine was nice, but Jap silk went hard after a few washings. The only mending I ever did myself was sometimes having a go at the pile of socks; Dick would get much attached to various immensely heavy country stockings.

The parlourmaid (or, with us, Lev and the parlourmaid together) waited at table, which had been carefully laid with the right cutlery and glasses and linen napkins folded into fans or mitres; I usually did the flowers or other decoration myself. They handed round the dishes for people to help themselves, offered wine (sometimes a choice), cleared plates, later brought the coffee tray through to the drawing room, where they had drawn the curtains, perhaps lighted a fire in a well-swept fireplace with polished fire irons. Above all, they washed up. Did we worry about being over-seen and overheard? Not a bit really, though I always said to leave us for cheese and dessert. One would find a hot water bottle in one's bed if that was appropriate, and in the morning a call with orange juice or tea for those who liked it. Breakfast would be there with letters and newspapers on the table and no remains of yesterday's party.

In the first years of my married life there was perennial border warfare between nursery and kitchen. This was general; when middle-class mums met sooner or later it came up for discussion. If there was a nursery maid, quite likely a bright girl in training for a better post, she was the go-between, the tray-carrier, the causer or smoother of difficulties. If nurse's meals were insufficient or not kept hot then there was trouble and usually the mistress was not brought in till there had already been bitter unforgettable words. The parlourmaid, who probably had her troubles in the kitchen, was usually on the nursery side, but with us Lev was bound to side with his wife.

The mother–nurse tension went deeper. Of course a nanny who had sole charge with the mother doing something altogether else—this was to some extent the high society pattern—simplified things for a time, though the partings were more painful in the end. What I wanted was a collaborator, an ally, a friend. This I finally got but not until Val was the baby in 1930. Mrs Davie (as she is now), whom later Val nicknamed Prits, was Highland, a MacRae from near Balmacarra with good radical views on social matters. She was in fact a trained nurse, but at that time more nurses were trained than hospitals could absorb so she had taken to the rather better-paid job of a children's nurse. She remembers getting about £6 a month but as she said to me, 'You'll be forgetting how many things one could get for £1 in those days.' She was always marvellously calm and sensible in any medical crisis, measles or scarlet fever, not to speak of Val crawling round the table and biting Avrion's leg or Avrion seeing things which were invisible to others. She comes into my book *We Have Been Warned*. Having her there made all the difference to me.

The Twenties and Thirties were a curious transitional period for women who were for a few decades free of the household chores which had been thought for so long to be women's work. Quite a number of women took advantage of this new freedom to write, paint, do scientific or historical research, become doctors, lawyers and so on. I was one. Clearly without domestic help I could not have had a family and been a successful writer. Is this a sufficient excuse for those who consider me and my friends as bourgeois capitalist exploiters? Certainly not.

But there is one other thing. I am fairly sure that my household staff were on the whole happy and felt they were doing a worthwhile job, skilled enough to be satisfying, not very arduous and more secure than many an industrial job at that time. I have discussed this since with intelligent women who were in domestic service, though today with more education they might have been in offices or shops. What mattered to them was that their mistress should be 'a lady'. What qualities did that imply? Being considerate, not putting on airs, willingness to help, patience, humour, but also some degree of apparent worth and leadership. Perhaps that was what it was all about.

So there we were and rooms were clean and tidy, the meals were cooked and served, orders to shops were delivered on time and there were at least three posts a day, all based on our being at the top end of the class structure. We could presumably have sat back and enjoyed it but we filled up all that lovely spare time which nobody seems to have today with our friends and children, ours and our friends' love affairs, our good causes and committees, Dick's Bar work, my writing, interest in the other arts, letters, trips abroad and as time went on the growth of social conscience. The last didn't go as far as doing without Lev, nurse, cook, housemaid and the rest, which would of course also have meant giving up our home, dependent as it was on them. But at least we found ourselves living into a frame of mind where the class structure began to look very unreal.

MATTERS OF LIFE AND DEATH

Another source of class distinction in the Twenties and Thirties was health. On the whole, good health was privilege: it belonged to the middle and upper classes. You have only to look at photographs of primary-school children from an industrial area or glance at statistics of height and weight class-wise. There were of course no such things then as free ante-natal and post-natal clinics, foot clinics, school dentistry and so on. People were used to suffering: it had been there for the whole of human history. My family and I belonged to the privileged, but that did not stop deaths which could easily have been averted by today's antibiotics.

Hospitals had been greatly improved and humanised by the experience of the 1914–18 war. Surgery, including anaesthetics and analgesics, had improved out of all knowledge. Vaccination had been going on for a century but during the Twenties other types of inoculation came in. When Murdoch got diphtheria he had the correct jab and so had the rest of my family and my grandmother at Cloan was quickly reassured. Her sixteen-year-old, a brilliant violinist, had died of diphtheria in the 1870s. But had we been in a lower income group the diphtheria might not have been diagnosed soon enough. Measles, diphtheria and tuberculosis above all pushed up the curve of the death rate, especially among the less well off. And if for example a family with a minor professional income had to support a relation in a sanatorium for months they could easily drop down to a lower level. To some extent hospital treatment was free but it was not exactly pleasant.

During this between-wars period most ordinary operations were done at home if the home was clean and roomy. Murdoch had his appendix out at Cherwell; he was at the Dragon School at the time and living with my parents. The children—and Dick—had their tonsils out at home. It was a case of scrubbing a wooden table, getting a new piece of mackintosh sheeting, having the few necessary utensils and plenty of confidence. A trained nurse came in for a few days; later on Nurse and I managed between us. I myself managed to escape the tonsil-cutting fashion but poor Dick, often somewhat bothered by sore throats, nearly had his out in Vallay off North Uist. Zadok the doctor was most enthusiastic about doing it there and then but the tide was coming in and if he didn't get away quickly across Vallay Strand he might be late for his next patient!

In 1927, when he was nine, our eldest son Geoff died of meningitis in a London nursing home. There is some description of what it was like in *Point Counter Point*. I do not now blame Aldous for writing about it; no doubt in the state I was in I clung on to any friends to tell them, tell them, force them to share. One recovers in a sense but never completely. One can look back beyond but never without pain, never without some shadow of possible guilt. The sum of pain in the world has been increased by that fraction; it does not balance with anything. It was very difficult for the other children to accept and bad for them; we all got over it, as they say, but somewhat maimed. And Geoff was and is dead.

Before that there had been, for me at least, a kind of security and comfort of mind, taken for granted. Life would have its ups and downs but the war was over and things were getting better everywhere—or so it appeared. We had more friends, more fun, we were out of danger. Progress would go on steadily. But progress had not got to the stage of antibiotics, and the specialists brought desperately in could do nothing. With antibiotics Geoff might have been alive today, thinking, presumably about his retirement plans after a life of—what? I still wince away, inevitably blaming myself, thinking if I had taken more trouble at the beginning when he first got ear-ache. If only. If only. There is no answer.

In Chelsea we had a jolly local woman doctor who came on call, sewed up cuts, diagnosed children's diseases, gave whatever medicines were appropriate and told us what quarantine times we must keep. These were much stricter than now but, as most of the diseases were that much graver, there was something

The author in court dress, with Lois, about 1926

Dick in the early 1920s

to be said for it. When I had scarlet fever the door was draped with a carbolic-soaked sheet. She was the 'family doctor', paid, I think, yearly; but for anything grave a specialist was called in. I know Dick's parents had a specialist to consult about his headaches and depressions, but I am fairly certain that it was all put down to his head wound and that the main drug used was some kind of bromide, the only treatment for those who were 'overwrought'. They had used paraldehyde on him when he was really delirious and violent in the military hospital; I can still remember the smell of it. I believe now that he had a genuine depression of the kind which can today be treated—more or less. He himself said that his state of mind was entirely due to not getting briefs, a not unusual experience for a young barrister. My own fits of post-natal depression never had any drugs prescribed for them, nor did they last. They were simply taken as normal and perhaps a makeweight for the hyperaesthesia which I always felt during pregnancy.

Dick had a bad cough one winter and his mother sent us both down to the Riviera for a week. There was light snow on the slopes and brilliantly fruiting arbutus bushes, but there were no other young people. At that time the Riviera was a winter retreat for the well-off elderly; there were no summer playgrounds yet. Winter coughs were usual: my brother and I both had them regularly. Heroin lozenges were the answer; they tasted sufficiently nasty to stop anyone getting addicted. Flu was taken seriously but those of us who had been through the 'Spanish flu' of 1918—and survived—were in little danger.

In the Thirties the sulpha drugs came into use: Rubiazol or something similar. Vitamins were just beginning to get used but the classification was much simpler and less accurate than today's. Probably they did some good to some people but before the National Health Service they certainly did not get to those who needed them most.

It is interesting to have lived through successive fashions of childbirth. In the early Twenties it was still thought of with some alarm and excitement; one was so to speak going into battle and for those who could afford it every possible ally was brought in. As far as I was concerned this meant a Harley Street specialist, a woman gynaecologist—I would have acutely disliked having a man. For the first three births I was at Oxford, later in London with dear Dr Pirret who died in the London blitz. Twice I had to have the position of the child reversed to avoid a dangerous presentation and this is a skilled bit of obstetrics. In addition to everyone else my mother was always present at the delivery, as by right, though I began to feel this a considerable embarrassment. Not unnaturally Dick felt somewhat in the way and tended to absent himself, nor was there any thought at the time of husbands being present.

I always had rather difficult confinements owing to pelvic distortion following my early broken femur and adaptation to a shortened leg. The babies were getting bigger and the difficulties increased, so the last births were induced two or three weeks before term. With only one of the babies was the birth process reasonably rapid or even at a sensible time of day. I always ended with chloroform, it was the usual anaesthetic at that period; one took a whiff on one's own from the mask or handkerchief when things got bad. Gradually one was allowed to increase it and finally one was all out. It is a delightful feeling of pain turning into warmth and falling stars. I was never given any of the modern pain-killers; in fact I doubt whether any of them existed. After chloroform I always came to quickly with no ill effect but somewhat excited, demanding to have the baby, unwashed, at once. Ergotamine was standard for the afterbirth.

Those in my social class had a monthly nurse at home after having a child—sometimes very nice and reassuring, sometimes a disruptive bully, always someone who had to be waited on. After my first child in 1918 I was in bed for nearly a fortnight, but I'd had a rather alarming ante-partum haemorrhage and afterwards mastitis with a good deal of fever and pain. In bed and also after I was allowed up I was swathed round the middle with a tight bandage. This was the last time that happened; but probably nurses, to whom this kind of thing was left, stuck to their rituals long after it was clear that they were medically pointless. By the same token, the baby was sewn into a flannel binder for two or three weeks—it was changed, of course—before progressing to a knitted cummerbund.

I only stayed in bed three or four days for the second birth, got up almost at once for the third, but after that went back to two or three days, thus exemplifying changing medical fashions. After a time the idea of post-partum exercises came in; at the same time the old rules about suitable diet for a nursing mother gave way, until finally I was encouraged to eat the fruit, including even oranges, which had been forbidden so firmly ten years earlier. Nor was I urged to drink 'nursing stout'. Of course the change had no effect on the baby's breast milk.

Weekly weighing of the baby was part of the ritual, and always caused some anxiety. Had the baby gained enough—or sometimes too much? We had our book—in those days Truby King, which meant four-hourly feeds, taking not more than twenty minutes, however slow a starter the baby was; and that baby must be allowed to cry if it stupidly began to be hungry before the clock struck. Nor must there be any stray pickings up and pettings except at the authorised play period. I don't know why all this was accepted, but worried mothers (and there were always plenty of people, both of an older generation and their own contemporaries, to worry them) have a habit of accepting authoritative books, by doctors.

It was only with Valentine that I threw Truby King out of the window; though she settled in to more or less four-hourly feeds after two or three months, she got a lot more picking up and cuddling. I also went on the idea that babies understand what is said, more than is apparent. If I was going out in the evening, and likely to be coming back a bit late for her last feed, I would lean over her cot beside my bed and tell her so, saying everything was all right, that she should just sleep until I came back. This seemed to work, and when I was there in the room again she would wake, smilingly punctual. I remember these drowsy comforting night feeds, and sometimes going to sleep and realising that I had long passed the Truby King limit, but to hell with that.

The babies' first food, other than mother's milk, varied with medical fashion. Avrion got veal bones, which he used to hit people with if possible, laughing till the milk bubbled out.

In spite of having babies, which is commonly supposed to tidy things up, I went on having menstrual pain and excessive bleeding. It was not taken seriously in those days. Probably there were no suitable drugs; after all it was a mere female problem and scarcely worthwhile for the drug houses to put time and trouble into. But by that time something else was happening for women which was going to be almost as important an agent of social change as the National Health Service. That was the birth-control movement, then mainly thought of as family spacing and helping in the emancipation of women, not as population control, still less as allowing general 'permissiveness'. Most of us would have been shocked at today's assumption that nice girls take the pill!

Before my marriage my mother had spoken vaguely of 'Malthusian capsules' which perhaps she had used herself. But I paid no attention, any more than I did to anything else she told me about the facts of life. However, in the Twenties, after the birth of our second child, I went and got fitted with a Dutch cap used with an ointment or pessary. For me this was easy and effective. It was the main method used at the North Kensington Clinic.

I was on the committee of the clinic, the first to be started after Marie Stopes's own—and she I fear only felt we were rivals and probably giving the wrong advice. On the other hand we all realised the importance of her work and especially her book *Married Love.* Marie Stopes was quite often at my parents' house, discussing the coal measures with my father. She was a colleague, a good palaeobotanist. If he ever heard her name linked with less acceptable subjects he paid no attention.

I wonder if we had completely thought out the changes all this was bound to make. Well, who does? Many of the North Kensington committee members had largish families, especially me and my cousin Margaret Maze. We were sometimes asked to volunteer for tests and information, largely under the direction and supervision of that great doctor Helena Wright; this could be embarrassing but somebody had to do it. We also helped at the clinic with interviews and filling in forms. It grew quickly along the lines of giving advice on other gynaecological problems.

There was also the money-raising side. For this we had a fancy dress ball in the Hammersmith Palais de Danse; I managed a splendid mediaeval dress with a hennin on my head which, as I was at the time fairly far advanced in pregnancy, was very becoming. We also did several of my children's plays. There was *Nix-Nought-Nothing* with lighting effects showing the fish and bird flocks beautifully; these were worked out by our architect neighbour, John Macgregor, whose daughters I am sure were in it. *Kate Crackernuts* was put on more professionally in the small Mercury Theatre at Notting Hill Gate. Avrion, then three, was the fairy baby who has to give Kate the wand and the cake. He knew this part and it suddenly occurred to him that all the others were allowed to talk—why not him? I said all right, for clearly it would have been useless to say anything else, but explained that it was part of the story. I thought he understood and indeed what he said was quite in character but not very audible. He looked entrancing, all in tinsel and blond curls.

THE DAILY ROUND

CHILDREN WERE A constant presence in the Hammersmith house, but the daily routine began, for me, at my desk. After we moved to River Court I had a succession of young and pretty secretaries, probably ill-paid, but they seemed to enjoy themselves and I always found myself sympathetically involved with their love lives. They also helped with domestic problems. When the current secretary turned up, probably around ten, we chatted, perhaps about the progress of her love affair, and dealt with letters; there were always a lot which could be answered by someone else or to which I could dictate a quick answer. (Remember we still wrote rather than telephoned.) There were all sorts of arrangements to be made, trains to look up and people to get hold of. In those days it was much more possible to get things mended, but one had to find the 'little man'; Dick was never as good round the house as a modern husband is expected to be and often is. A good deal of the work was actually to do with my writing and a letter to Lewis Gielgud about some play we were hatching up might take several detailed pages. I wrote my books spasmodically, then as now often on journeys. This might mean a long session of dictation. If it was something I had typed myself there might be quantities of alterations. Then there might be London Library books to sort out.

Sometimes I lunched out with friends, sometimes they came to me. It wasn't expensive unless one chose to make it so. The Café Royal in the big room with the plush benches gave one lunch for half a crown, including coffee and, I think, a glass of wine. But once I went there with my pretty cousin Christine and was told that they couldn't have two ladies coming in without a gentleman. I was furious and stormed at them: 'Do you take me for a tart?'

'I'm sure I couldn't say, Miss,' was the answer.

Often enough one of the children had to be taken to get shoes, or perhaps to the dentist or to afternoon classes. Eurhythmics were the thing then. Denny at seven was a pleasure to watch—at least for me. He went off to school and dropped it at once, but the others followed on. There were gym classes too. I myself went to Miss Parkinson's, often taking the children—was their class after or before mine? We trotted round, jumped over the horse, did parallel bars and single bar balance, the lot. I never could climb a rope properly and it worried me. But one night I dreamt I could and the next day I went shinning up, my feet and ankles remembering the dream.

During the day there were plenty of other things to do in London—exhibitions, occasionally demos in the later Thirties. Avrion loved these and did splendid bang-bang pictures afterwards, though we were never really in a bang-bang area. Demos and marches were very peaceable by modern standards. May Day was great fun, a family affair; we used to march quite a long way with bands and banners. In the United Front days Val was lured off by the local Communists to help sell the *Daily Worker* and collect for the Party. Various comrades lifted her up to collect from windows along the smarter parts of the Bayswater Road; she was very successful. Then we all had sandwiches in the park.

And if I was out the children were having a safe and cheerful time with Nurse, if it was fine out in the garden or round about. On wet days there was the big rocking horse in the bay window looking over the river, books and bricks and toys. Nurse always kept a few specials in the locker under the other window, which they couldn't open; these would come out fresh. Lois was the reader. Avrion was the wild one, with his dreams and apparitions, not seen by anyone else.

However, if Mr Booker, our once-a-week gardener, was there, Avrion was no problem. He followed Mr Booker's wheelbarrow endlessly, asking questions all the time. He and Nurse had found some deserted mallard ducklings, which they brought up, building them a duck house in a corner of the garden; when they were old enough they were taken to Virginia Water and let loose. But Avrion had a lion cub which had become increasingly ragged and dirty and unrecognisable to anyone but its owner, who needed it especially at night. Once it got left in the garden and all of us had to go and hunt for it with torches while its owner howled our heads off. Ours was the biggest local garden, with space for hide-and-seek, and there were often quite a lot of children in from round about.

What fun it all sounds, so much livelier and more interesting than the life we lead now, above all so much less tiring, when other people were doing most of the tedious chores. But of course we got bored and cross; I often got madly impatient with the children, about nothing much, I'm sure, and found myself hurling the telephone book at one or the other, though it always missed. I had difficulties with my mother, was unnecessarily nasty to her and then felt bad about it.

And I combined feelings of guilt about our capitalist situation with occasional envy of those who had yachts and heated swimming pools surrounded by palm trees, who were eighteen when I was thirty-eight, who did genuinely dangerous and noble things or were actually best-sellers. In fact I behaved normally.

And all the time the book or poem I was writing would be flowering at the back of my mind, a tasting of words, a slow-motion film waiting only to be written down. And I wrote anywhere: in the Underground—sometimes I took a turn round the Circle Line if I wanted to finish something uninterrupted. In the British Museum or at the dentist's. Or of course at home, where there were constant interruptions, some interesting, others not and often made entirely by myself.

Writing or not, the children came down for drawing-room tea with clean faces and hands and I read to them afterwards, though it was difficult to find a book for all ages and the younger ones got bored. In winter we had our crumpets toasted at the fire and dripping with butter whenever we could; one of the boys went rushing out when we heard the muffin man's bell coming down Rivercourt Road. There was a River Court mouse that used to come out and eat our crumbs, but one day we made a plate of incompetent toffee that didn't set and the poor mouse got stuck and had to be picked out; after that it was too frightened to visit us again. I also managed to play the tunes of nursery rhymes on the piano with one hand and we all sang them together. I hate to think what kind of noise we must have made!

Often Nurse and I bathed the children together and I usually said them poems after they were in bed. I am not sure if they liked this but perhaps it gave them a feeling for words and rhythm. We gave the smallest ones their supper—usually just bread and milk, and perhaps an apple for all of them. This was the accepted thing and they'd had a solid tea, but by today's standards it was rather meagre and might be short on protein. But there were extras. In winter nursery toast could be made at any time if one reached over the guard and poked till there was a nice layer of glowing coals. There was butter, there was jam and fish paste and golden syrup and cheese and apples. Nurse sometimes fried herself onions on the gas ring in the bathroom and doubtless the children had a taste.

In those days in our kind of family those under ten never came down to dinner with the grown-ups. Children's bedtime was between six and eight, though as they got older they read in bed. They probably woke earlier than children now, but that was Nurse's job, not mine. And it meant that the evening was for grown-ups. I had a bath and changed. Dick got back after seven and usually changed too; even when we were alone we would be in some kind of evening dress. Sometimes he told the children stories, making them up as he went along. These were very good and I wrote down some of them. Naturally the children themselves came into them and often the first dog, Cobweb.

If we were going out to dinner I was usually ready in time. I didn't take that long because somehow I had never learnt how to put on make-up so I didn't use it. I did try once, but the family agreed I looked awful. Over the years it is quite a saving! I got my hair cut and set occasionally, but normally depended on a good brushing. Dick used to give me scent as a birthday present, Chanel's No. 6. I didn't like him to give me expensive presents, especially jewellery, though he sometimes did, and always it was something special and beautiful.

Just occasionally we were asked to a white-tie party, though

I can't remember ever giving one, and then I had to try and find long white gloves, which I could at least dangle. The big parties we were asked to would either be studio parties or else the occasional embassy party. Our friends on the whole gave the same parties as ourselves—nice houses, not very interesting food, probably one or two new faces. We were back and in bed by midnight.

Occasionally we went to films or more often to the theatre. Once in the Albert Hall there was a glorious mixed occasion, a full orchestra playing the *Ring* music, while the silent screen showed a magnificent German film of the earlier version of the story, with beautiful, blonde, naked boys and girls, horses and bulls and savage scenery. Could one repeat that now? The Lyric Theatre in Hammersmith was doing fairly well; there was a long run of *The Beggar's Opera* which I managed to get to several times and once one of the Russian Ballet visits. Karsavina was dancing in the *Spectre de la rose* and wanted a beautiful chair. They asked me if I could lend one and I was thrilled and brought it round myself; there was Karsavina, her face ageing, but her body muscles clearly those of a young athlete. I was so happy that she was pleased with my chair.

Most evenings when we were just ourselves at home we were probably both writing letters for the late post or I might be checking and signing what my secretary had left. The last post went at nine and it was a pleasure to walk along the Embankment in the quiet evening as far as the pillarbox with the grey river rippling along at our left hand. We might even walk on up river and look in on some of the neighbours.

There was plenty to talk about—especially, of course, in later years the constituency. Or on my side trouble with Mrs Levinson or one of the others. Or schools. A new school was said to be starting which would have modern ideas like a children's council and a parents' association. Would this be worth following up? Or what was really happening in Germany? Surely it couldn't be true? Or could it?

EDUCATION AND OUR PRINCIPLES

HOW DID OUR political principles affect something very important —the education of our children? I had taken one look at the nearest primary school in Hammersmith, a church school, and was horrified: it was grubby and smelly and the children would have hated it. Agreed, primary education had to be upgraded, but until it was —no. In Scotland at least it was usual for all local children, whatever their parents' circumstances, to go to the village primary school; after that, if there was a good grammar school as there were in many Scottish towns, they would go there, though some went on to the famous fee-paying Edinburgh and Glasgow day schools, such as the Edinburgh Academy, where my father went. But in upper-middle-class England the structure was different. It was taken for granted that children should leave home quite young, especially boys. We were sometimes criticised for keeping our sons at home until they were nine years old. It would be bad for their characters, soften them. And of course I remembered how much I myself had wanted to go away to school. I hated losing them, but felt it was the right thing to do.

Murdoch had a disastrous couple of terms at a Dorset prep school supposed to be in a particularly salubrious part of Britain, experiencing the nastiness of small boys to one another, but they all went on to the Dragon School at Oxford where many of the pupils were quite civilised; it was chosen partly no doubt on pressure from my mother, as the boys stayed at Cherwell, my parents' home, which was only five minutes' walk away from the school and where they and their young Dragon friends had the run of the fields and hedges and chestnut trees. The boys certainly had a very good time there and played quite a lot in the laboratory, since my father in his old age was working less there and more in the study among his immensely heaped papers.

But the next stage? Dick and my brother had both been to

Eton and had at least done very well there academically. The boys were put down for Eton shortly after their birth. This was quite usual. Eton was said to be, and probably was, much broadened and more progressive. Aldous Huxley had taught there (of course with no teaching qualifications, but he was an old Etonian!). And several bright young rebels had sprung from Eton's paternal loins.

But how did it square with other ideas, and what about the way my brother had been bullied? It might be all right perhaps in college or as an Oppidan scholar but Denny, terribly shaken by Geoff's death, had slipped academically to a point where he would certainly not have done well enough in common entrance and at Eton would be placed far too low for his real abilities. So after a while I said, 'I'd like to go and see what it's like now.' I went with Dick and felt very uncomfortable, as perhaps did the housemaster and dame. We talked about health, attitudes towards religion and politics, some aspects of teaching and also of sex; I looked with disfavour at the large cars which were standing around outside School Yard and felt myself being somewhat disapproved of. I came away saying 'Over my dead body'. I couldn't stand the mixture of privileged snobbery and firm religious indoctrination—all boys going to confirmation classes. They were still wearing those awful stuffy clothes! No doubt many aspects are better now, but equally our principles are sharper and doubtless our incomes are smaller.

So then we started looking for alternatives, some, such as Bryanston, attractive in many ways. At one school the headmaster said, 'There is no sex in my school.' That went off the list. We didn't have to worry about drugs and knew that at most schools a firm line was taken on drink and cigarettes; at home our older ones would have a glass of wine with us at dinner.

We finally chose Abbotsholme, mostly because of Sharpe, the headmaster, who was making the school into something we deeply approved of, was likely to be particularly understanding about Denny and help him to get back his intellectual and moral confidence. The staff were young, friendly and full of ideas, it was in beautiful country. They did encourage Denny, treat him well and give him lots of freedom. Music appreciation and teaching were first-class. No doubt academic standards would have been higher at Eton, but he might not have learned how to wire a small theatre with adequate stage lighting and I am sure some schools would have disapproved of his close friendship with another boy. At any rate it was probably less of a mistake than most parental choices.

Murdoch however wanted to go to a proper public school. This was probably the influence of the Dragon School; also, I expect, of my mother. After some hesitation Dick said he could go to Winchester—but it must be college. We did not think much of the house system. He duly got his scholarship and was I think immediately surprised at the civilised behaviour of the other boys. On the whole he was extremely happy; this was partly due to two outstandingly sympathetic masters, James, later at York, and Lucas. Winchester is a marvellously beautiful place; élitist no doubt, but they looked after the pupils' health and Dick Gleadowe was an inspiring craftsman, though his ideal was exquisite pencil work and he looked down on Murdoch's bookbinding. But his house was open and friendly. There must also have been good science teaching for that period. It was there that we met three beautiful lads, John Sparrow, Dick Crossman and perhaps Richard Wilberforce.

But then it was Lois's turn. We had thought it would be a good idea for her to be away from home and sent her for a year to St Christopher's. It was vegetarian and gave her a permanent dislike for cheese. If we had known how much she hated it we would have taken her away. But parents never do know. After that we hunted round, equally disliking most of what we saw. Then I met that great old girl, Miss Baker, and was much impressed (Mark Arnold-Forster's mother, Ka, was even more impressed by Hahn and sent Mark to Gordonstoun which was probably all wrong for him). At least Badminton was not vegetarian, though it was a stronghold of cultural liberalism. School report had it that B & B, as the headmistress was nicknamed, washed Gilbert Murray's pants for him. It was a tribute to the League of Nations, of which by this time he was one of the strongest supporters.

You may well ask how all this élitist education and Oxbridge taken for granted at the end of it, squares with Labour Party ideals. It doesn't, of course. The whole thing is a compromise, between educational ideals, including freedom, constant intellectual and aesthetic stimulation and awareness, and an ability to be part of the real world. Whatever schools are like, there is no real equality and not much fraternity, so long as one child comes from a home with books, telly and radio used not as background noise but for furthering knowledge and appreciation, intelligent adult conversation he is allowed to join in, while another child comes from a home with none of these things. So it is more than education which needs changing.

BUYING THINGS

WHAT DID WE buy? What did we wear, what did we eat? What was our taste in china, pictures, decoration, books, everything?

Much depends on technology and available energy, for example for domestic heating. In the Twenties and early Thirties most people wore wool next the skin for eight months of the year, and from those who could not afford frequent washing with hot water and soap came the smell of a London crowd or a primary school. My woolly vests and knickers, replacing the horrible combinations and even thicker knickers of my childhood, were frequently washed, though not by me. In the early Twenties no female wore a bra; we had to be flat, a slightly awkward fashion for a nursing mother. Over my woollies I wore, in winter, a tweed skirt and Shetland jersey, or a woollen dress; in summer I often wore a smock or pinafore dress with a cotton shirt. We didn't wear trousers or tights. Stockings were dull, not much variety in shoes, but I kept one solid pair with my skates permanently fastened on to them. Most years there seemed to be skating somewhere. Virginia Water was lovely, long stretches and few people; I never did figure skating but loved just whirling along.

Pretty maternity dresses came out several times before finally lapsing into the acting box. There was a green velvet with short panels at the sides and a big tying bow of primrose crêpe de Chine. A green silk had a crinkly, semi-transparent slip and a gold-embroidered overdress to go with it; another was blue silk. Clothes were cotton, silk, wool, or mixtures and in each textile every kind of grade; a fine lisle stocking with silk clocks was nicer than pure silk. My mother-in-law occasionally took me to Bradley's, an expensive shop which went in for velvets and brocades; once she gave me a fur coat but I didn't like it much. But at first I had little idea of what suited me and didn't manage at all well. She herself got most of her clothes from one of the big *couturières*, Worth, I think. But I doubt if I ever wanted that; it was clearly a nuisance, what with getting the right shoes, hat and accessories.

Children's clothes were much more of a temptation; small boys still wore hand-finished smocks or tunics. English children's clothes were much admired and sought after on the Continent, though later other countries developed their own styles. The very first children's jeans we ever saw were Danish, a present from Sonja Carstensen (later Meyer) in 1933, bright red cotton with brass buckles; three-year-old Val loved them.

Seasonal clothes were the same for children; in winter they wore knitted woolly coats and leggings with an elastic under the shoe which was probably a bit uncomfortable. Before and after pretty-dress parties they were immensely wrapped up with shawls and Shetland coatlets which sometimes had to stay on. We didn't expect warm rooms; woollen twin sets were worn indoors. Schoolchildren expected chilblains in most winters. A house might have warmed up by evening if fires had been lit in time, but it was as well to have a shawl over one's evening dress and probably a woolly vest under it, pinned down at the neck so as not to show. But by the mid-Thirties central heating had become almost usual in the kind of houses we went to. Then how lovely to get into cotton or silk and fine linen for four months of summer! Even the furniture dressed differently, with fresh cotton summer covers. Warm houses have taken some of the seasonal interest out of clothes, just as the deep freeze has done for fruit and vegetables. But perhaps we overdo it. And perhaps we may have to regress.

Dick, naturally, went to a good London tailor for the discreet suits which were *de rigueur* for a young barrister. A black topper for funerals and a grey one for weddings. It was all I could do to get him out of a stiff shirt and into a ruffled soft one to go with his dinner jacket, though tails still meant a stiff shirt and white tie which I used to help with organising. But gradually he began to allow himself short-sleeved linen shirts for playing squash and country holidays, in bright, plain colours. Both of us wore silk pyjamas in bed, blue or white or bright red usually.

The only time I was an avid hat buyer was early in our Chelsea years when there was a hat shop in Sloane Street with a baby chimpanzee. It came and chatted, put its arms round my neck, picked up little bits of feather or trimming in delicate fingers and was to me worth the money I spent on a hat. When it left for some zoo I never bought another hat there—in fact, except for occasional weddings, I rarely bought another hat; my long hair, done up in plaits and two earphones, didn't suit hats. But later, in the Thirties, whenever I went to Paris I bought two painter's *feutres*, one for myself, another for Wyndham Lewis. He wore his all the time, indoors and outdoors, so he wore them out fast.

Later on I was more assured about dress. I was stock-size or, if a small alteration was needed, any of the big shops did it cheaply, quickly and willingly; expecting service, we got it. It is sad to have missed today's fashions, many of which would have suited me then, though they don't now, for it would be such very elderly mutton dressed as lamb. But bikinis, ethnics, low-cut and sleeveless dresses would have been just my things; I had practically no armpit hair. Some of my nicest clothes were low-waistline linen dresses in the Augustus John fashion. I got smocks for the children and myself at the big Women's Rural Institute exhibition which was held in London every year and once a splendid bedspread made out of individually embroidered squares, which lasted a long time even with babies rampaging on it. I often got material for the children's dresses from Liberty's and Nurse really enjoyed making them up, though the girls didn't like trying them on.

For a couple of years I used to get rather nice, arty summer dresses from a lady who ran a kind of boutique and persuaded several of her friends or customers to put in a few hundred pounds each. Then she went elegantly bankrupt, appearing in court in black gloves and a very smart outfit, while we, her creditors, got a minimal amount back.

I almost always got my evening dresses made by a marvellous Swedish friend, Anna Sturge, who lived in the Temple—her husband was a distinguished lawyer. She made me dresses with beautiful embroidery symbols which we devised between us, including the dew-pearled rose which she put with some laughter round the waist of a Spring Queen dress—these would get past the censor! I wore this with a coloured band in my hair that dripped yellow silk corn ears; at that time my hair was ripe corn-coloured. It was always such fun going to see her and talking literature in a serious continental way among her beautiful bits of material, piled on chairs or all over the floor, oh so different from the dressmakers of my childhood. Nor did her dresses ever seem to date, as shop dresses did, though the silk is now very frail.

Shopping for food became more interesting over the between-wars years. I was very cautious at first. If we had guests for dinner I felt we had to have four courses, something like clear soup, fried sole, roast chicken with peas and duchesse potatoes, and some creamy pudding. Chicken was party food with a very definite flavour, not just broiler meat. It was dearer than beef or mutton, and game in season was about the same. Fish was poor locally but good and cheap in the big shops. From inshore fishing boats it got to London much faster than it does now, unfrozen and fresh. Fish fingers were for the future.

The kind of 'good, plain cook' I had was not imaginative but knew a few simple rules as well as having the upper hand of any young wife. She would be unwilling to try anything new: 'Oh, you couldn't expect me to look at that, madam!' No reputable pre-war newspaper would have dreamed of publishing recipes and the women's magazines had hardly started. Rather too often our food turned out to be not very nice. Something was burnt or under-done and I didn't know enough to complain intelligently or explain to the cook what she was doing wrong. She would of course have had no use for continental cooking. Except for curry in a few Anglo-Indian homes, rice was little used except for milk puddings, which still went on, though I'd had to consume so many unwillingly that I rarely gave them to my own children, who, in consequence, quite liked them. But I did expect the cook to make scones or a plain cake most days. She and I both tended to think of meat always in terms of hot roast; cold; rissoles or shepherd's pie; then start again.

Housekeeping, however, was not nearly so difficult after World War One as it was after World War Two. Rationing was soon dropped and business as usual, the great World War One slogan, saw to it that the 'usual' was available for those who could pay for it. Gradually I began to think up a few alternatives for the kitchen. I began going to the Army & Navy Stores or Harrods, to order what I wanted, which was of course delivered on the dot by one of their vans. I was recognised in their fruit departments as a customer for imported fruit, red bananas, the new grapefruit, blood oranges, grapes and tangerines. Pineapples and melons were for best and might cost as much as half a crown. But we could get named English dessert apples, whatever we asked for, at a few pence a pound and that even at smaller shops. There was always a summer glut of fruit, each at its season; even in London we made jam. There were lots of nice greengrocers in the King's Road, but not one delicatessen.

At River Court my standards of suitable food went up a bit. I would now order a pair of pheasants and the cook must be sure to make proper game chips and fried bread triangles for the pheasants to sit on; I would look round Harrods for interesting vegetables, and of course fresh watercress. And there must be plenty of lemons for the children's lemonade. The staff tended to finish things off and expected a fair amount of meat, but I did not oversee their catering. They had their main meal in the middle of the day, when, if I was alone, I fiddled around with fruit and cheese and nuts, and went on reading or writing. I'm sure Jessie or that jolly Irish girl who married the milkman might have said: 'We're having a nice jam roll for ourselves and the nursery. I'll send up a bit for you.' But if the older children were back from school, they would be eating with me, especially when we had lunch out in the garden and Clym the Bedlington puppy and Tuppence the black kitten or Peter the rabbit would turn up for a bite.

I never bought wine or even cider. That was strictly a man's job. We had a reasonably good cellar, especially for ordinary table wine, which Dick bought straight from France. Once we went walking in the Ardennes with the older boys, quite strenuous but with intervals of wine-tasting with the wine merchants who were often ex-*poilus*, so that Dick's experience with the French army came in well. There was talk about the wine itself, jokes about the 'crocodiles', as any little bits floating in the wine were called. So seeing the label later on recalled the pines, the walk down from the mountains, the vine-flower smell of the great, cool cellars, the splendid sleepifying dinners. However, some of the better wine came from Berrys or from wine auctions.

We had adequate local shops in Hammersmith, but if I was going shopping in town my great pleasure was bookshop browsing, which I had started at Oxford. My favourite place was of course Bumpus, the old one in Oxford Street with the back entrance. Here I could graze about among the newest writers. Often I visited Mr Wilson in his den between the crowded shelves of the books he really liked. He was constantly encouraging, often with excellent critical judgement, telling me about the books I ought to be reading or what was likely to be good and worth reviewing when it came out. He and Aunt Bay were great friends with much in common; even their voices took on further Scottish overtones when they were talking to one another. He made Bumpus into a kind of club for book writers and readers and would even produce a wee dram for a good author in a black mood. But I went to other bookshops too, including Blackwells in Oxford where I had an account for many years. It always seemed to me a good idea to have an account with as many bookshops as possible, for one never knew when one mightn't need a book. And there was none of this nonsense about monthly accounts.

When we went abroad we bought things for our house: a green Venetian glass chandelier and glass candlesticks to go with it, an inlaid chest of drawers from the Scandinavian section of an international exhibition, Swedish and Italian chairs, Danish table glass, painted Norwegian children's furniture, or, from Paris, etchings by Merion and a little marble church carving. Other furnishings came from antique shops or auctions; there was a shop in Burford and a hatter's in Bath where we got the flower plates which I had later round the walls of my Carradale kitchen. None of these things were desperately expensive and such as I or the children still have seem not to have dated in taste. There was a lovely Chinese warehouse in the City where we occasionally bought things. But my own desk was by Gordon Russell, English oak designed to my specification and still of course with every drawer running perfectly. Then there were our Hammersmith friends, painters, sculptors, wood engravers; they too decorated our house.

It didn't seem out of the way during these years to get a book rebound or to go to some trouble to get glasses or cups to match a set. Powells engraved some wine glasses to match the family nineteenth-century ones, so well that I now can't tell which are which. I got myself sandals made at what became later a shop so expensive I wouldn't go near it. But at that time it was not easy to get a simple classical sandal ready made and hand-making was not that much dearer.

There were other specialists whom we went to, for instance Baldwins, the coin dealers, such nice people who hadn't then, as they do now, to live behind a burglar-proof barricade. Dick gave me Greek coins to match the period I was writing about, and I have kept them in a silver filigree box which he bought in Vicenza during his time in Italy in 1918. He had a little leather case made to fit inside it; that kind of thing could easily be done.

He got Sothebys' catalogues regularly and occasionally Christies'. We went usually together whenever anything interested us particularly. This way Dick got some fairly valuable china and a few Renaissance medals. I got—for shillings—Peruvian or Cypriot pots and no doubt bid for and failed to get things which would have appreciated still more in value. This was great fun, but I became more and more surprised at the difference between aesthetic and cash values. Downright ugliness was no bar to eager bidding. Dick knew much more about it than I did, though I was developing a taste and judgement for modern pictures and artefacts. Thirty years later this was useful in helping Argyll with their first-class travelling art exhibition for schools.

One of the places I used to go to in the Twenties was the Omega Workshops, where I sometimes bought interesting materials, and met, but only marginally, painters such as Roger Fry and Vanessa Bell. I bought various boxes, not always very well made, lamp standards and so on. The lampshades were particularly attractive, but the silk was too thin and rotted away very quickly, and Omega went in a little too much for casual spots and blotches. I also got them to design and make for me the really beautiful and well-finished dressing table, inlaid with grey and purplish wood on a cream-coloured background and with the Omega sign in the middle, which I had in my bedroom at River Court. It dated rather quickly and the time came when I had no use for a dressing table. So it has now gone to a museum.

There were lots of specialist shops in London, especially a lovely theatrical one in Seven Dials, where one could get almost everything: animal masks, crowns and coronets, every kind of sew-on decoration, and well-made fairy wings—I gave a pair to Val for her birthday one year, it was what she most wanted.

Fancy dress of any kind was much more popular in those days; it may come back if ever fashion swings away from the present idea that anything goes, so we can always and everywhere be in fancy dress. I was very much interested in the clothes which the characters in my historical books wore and how they must have felt in them, so I made myself a Doric chiton which is simply a piece of very wide cloth pinned on the shoulders and open down one side, though belted. I went to a party once in this, which was no doubt rather shocking for that period, though I expect I wore knickers. Yet of course the main dressing-up always goes on in the mind: Av and Val playing sabre-toothed tigers and every now and then it gets too much and Val rushes away: 'Don't want to be etten!'

Of course we had a Christmas tree every year. At River Court it stood, tier on green tier, just clear of the high ceiling of the drawing-room bay, where everyone passing could admire it through uncurtained windows. Decorating the tree I felt elevated, delighted. There were real candles, probably two boxes of them, all-coloured or gleaming white. I had some of the old candle-holders with clips and bought some even better adjustable ones.

It was a case of careful weighting of the branches to get a good and above all safe place for each candle. I did the top one from a stepladder while the children did the lower branches, re-living the pleasure of my own childhood. Every year we bought a few more of the lovely glass decorations, the birds with quivering spun-glass tails, the hollow brilliances, doorways into fairy worlds. Before the candles were lit I saw to it that there was a bucket of water and a heavy blanket, and I kept one eye on the tree all the time ready to catch any errant flame. Not once did we have more than a twig momentarily flaring and always there was the marvellous smell which I miss so much today of hot pine needles and candle smoke.

Small presents might hang on the tree, colour-wrapped chocolates in gold mesh bags, tiny wooden animals, paper blow-outs and crackers. The real presents were in the stockings, unless they were too big and had to be laid on the floor beside the bed. All the children did Dick's stockings, later on the older ones did mine. There might be some swapping!

As it happens I have exact notes of my Christmas shopping on 13 December 1937. At that time Mass Observation were asking us all to keep a diary one day a month and I have not only my own diary but a diary which Valentine, then aged seven, dictated to me, so I have a check on my own accuracy. My own diary starts in the afternoon at 2.45, when my son Denny, who had recently got a driving licence,

> drives me and Valentine to Kensington High Street Woolworths to get presents for Christmas Tree Party. Very wet day. Woolworths crowded largely with people wandering about looking at things. Whilst son is parking car Valentine and I get presents for him (pencil rubber) [this must have been Valentine's present because I certainly got him something much more special!]. Then get pencils, sweets and games for hanging on tree. While choosing sweets assistant asked twice 'Is this your little girl?' and beamed at Valentine. Several times I ask if goods are Japanese, but assistants don't seem to know. Can't hear what other people are saying, too much

noise. . . . Valentine chooses handkerchiefs for other brother and housemaid.

Four o'clock. Go on to Daniel Neal's, get blue shoes for Valentine, who knows what size she takes. Valentine knows routine of shops, gazes for a long time at her toes in the X-ray machine, wiggling them. Not very full. Toys displayed. A small child, five or so, says 'I'd like one of those trains for Christmas'. Mother says she doesn't know what he's going to get. Ask for Austrian knitted slippers for present. They only have size 6. I am sure my friend takes 7. Girl tries to persuade me they are all right. Then says she will telephone to other shop. Comes back saying they have them and she will send them off the next day. Valentine, bored, sprawls over a shoe trying-on stool, then on the floor. Denny tells her to get up. Back to car and home.

You will notice that we hadn't then understood that machines for X-raying children's feet might be dangerous. I then go on to say what they had for tea: 'Children have milk, hot flapjacks with butter, brown bread and butter, paste and jam. There is fruit salad, remains of yesterday's supper, for them, but they eat so much that they don't want it. Valentine has a bit of pineapple from yesterday. Denny has tea and flapjacks but fewer. I have tea with lemon, nothing else.'

Valentine's own account starts in the same place:

We went to Woolworths, with my brother driving, to buy some things. Mother just went out to see if the car was there; I stayed in Woolworths. . . . We bought some pencils and things which cost a penny and sixpence and tuppence. Then we saw Denny and Mother said something about a few minutes and we bought some chocolate things that she saw in the window . . . as well as some great big boxes of chocolates. We bought some candles, boxes of different colours . . . we stopped at Daniel Neal's to buy some shoes, pale blue ones to match my new dress for me and a pair of Austrian slippers because my mother had some and everybody liked them so much that she thought she would give some as a present. They had to ring up then to see if they could get the size and they were such a long time. . . . We went out and joined Denny and went home. Then we had tea with a lot of flapjacks and did some crackers, made a cracker trough, and counted out the things we had bought in dozens and did lots of other things. Everything was all right and we went to bed.

Before Christmas we always drove out into the country to get holly and ivy; there was still plenty for everyone. But mistletoe had to be bought, as well as oranges and red-cheeked apples. Tangerines could be threaded through with a needle for weighting tree branches; we always bought a box of them with little tinsel flowers between the fruit. The big Riviera boxes of pale thin wood for crystallised fruit might have tinsel flowers too. We had our fill of chestnuts. For the party I usually bought six or eight boxes of crackers from the Army & Navy; four dozen boxes were a good buy at about twelve shillings. We laid a couple at each place of the party table, which was a sit-down tea with sandwiches, small cakes and jellies.

The party was usually on Boxing Day, starting around 3.30. It was a genuine children's party, with at least a sprinkling of minders—mothers, nannies, older sisters and so on, all to be fed and given tea but not to sit at the table. There were all the cracker-grabbers, and those who didn't like them could if they were young enough be plucked out of their chairs and taken out of the bombardment. Meanwhile the extra-brave souls stood there sparking snaps out of other people's plundered crackers. The indoor fireworks were the best, with those lovely snakes' eggs, but possibly poisonous and only to be set alight when everyone had finished eating. It was a gorgeous mess afterwards of transparent wrappings through which to look at a world coloured green or red or blue, and stick-on pictures for putting into scrapbooks, pink icing and crumbs and mottoes, discarded hats or even ones still rolled up, and the smell of food and snaps.

No child went away empty-handed and I always kept a few

blow-outs or cardboard trumpets too high on the tree for casual grabbing, just in case. We played singing games or Hunt the Slipper and General Post, while the very small crawled or sat in the corners and played earnestly with their new things. Around 6 or 6.30 our guests were bundled into their warm coats and we brushed the floor. But the tree was still beautiful and the scent still hung in the Christmas air.

THE GREEN BOOK

IT WAS ON a top shelf out of reach. A blank book re-bound in a greeny-yellow Twenties paper with a leather label saying *River Court*. I lifted it down and there it all was. At one end I had listed all the parties we had after November 1923, when we moved to Hammersmith from Cheyne Walk. At first I had signatures of guests, but soon gave that up. At the other end were careful lists of people, changed every few years—couples, single men and single women with crosses at one side to show how often we had invited them, at the other side rather fewer crosses showing how often they had invited us. The Boat Race party had a big B and almost everybody had been asked. I was methodical about it and needed to be, at a time when hospitality was rather easier but much less casual than it is now. I didn't count neighbours dropping in, but I think they did it rather seldomer than they do in W11 where I now feel myself at home. Though certainly the Boat Race day meant general hospitality all along the river front with people moving from party to party, so that we often didn't recognise some of our own guests. I dream quite often about Boat Race parties but not of the race itself which I never saw much of because I had to keep an eye on the more excitable guests. Only once did one of them fall through the glass roof of a kind of ancient ground-floor passage. But he was one of the uninvited and anyhow wasn't hurt. Nowadays the parties, with the blue-ribboned crowds, are over, and we watch on telly instead; but it's less fun.

When I look at the lists of possible guests I find by 1936—the last time I brought the book up to date—perhaps a hundred couples and some sixty single men and women with a separate list of children. With the list of parties are comments: 'Not bad', 'Alpha plus I think', 'Nice—Juliette liked by all' (the first time Julian Huxley brought his young wife), 'All nice but somehow it didn't click, I can't think why', 'Awful argument', 'Fair to rain',

'Feminism?', 'Unexpectedly v.g.i.', 'Good but we had to drive back people late!', 'Damned hard work'. It looks as though we had three or four dinner parties a month, at any rate during the time when we were in London, but not in August or September. In later years, however, we had fewer dinner parties and more large informal ones. In June 1936 I have a note for one of these: 'About 130 accepted, 118 at least came—probably v.g. party.' But in April 1939 the ominous note is 'There was a sound of revelry by night' and for the last party of all, in July 1939, 'Dick had sore feet, I had a temperature and several people were drunk'.

I can usually read the names or nicknames of the people invited but sometimes I didn't even list them. In February 1934 there was simply 'A No More War movement party', or a list of invited names ending 'Plus lots of NFRB' (this being the New Fabian Research Bureau). For the Boat Race parties I tended to give out on names, just putting in *circa* 200–250. These big parties were easier to organise in some ways but one had to beware of strange social problems: for instance Wyndham Lewis, as always wearing his huge black hat, walking purposefully round apparently examining everybody but saying nothing, then just as purposefully walking out, leaving an immense question mark behind him.

Clearly there must have been frequent political differences. In 1936 I see on my lists the Pritts, John and Celia Strachey, the Ewers, Amyas Ross, Laski, Harry and Joan Thompson, the Nevinsons, Jeeves and Darling, Michael Foot, John Parker, Rudi Messel—but he was a peacemaker—Fenner Brockway, Barbara Betts, Reg Reynolds, then three together—Ellen Wilkinson, Dorothy Woodman, Madeline Symons—and of course Coles, Postgates, Beales and Horrabins: all lefties, from the Communist Party through to right-wing Labour or Liberal left. It could have been an explosive mixture though perhaps I tried to separate them.

There are not very many writers in the lists, other than those whose letters I have and about whom I shall be writing, but the local painters, by then including Julian Trevelyan and Len Lye, are there and, surprisingly, Benjamin Britten. I expect Margie Spring Rice brought this promising young man who was to be the star of the Festival at Aldeburgh, which was her home ground. By that time our friends the Spring Rices had parted company and only Margie remains at the beginning of the women's list. In April 1938 I notice Krishna Menon and Miss Nehru at a Boat Race party. Bernal came sometimes and Malinowski, but otherwise, apart from old friends like Julian Huxley, hardly anyone in the scientific world unless one counts Norman Haire, with his enormous stomach bulge under which a child carrying round sandwiches might be trapped. Towards the end I see not only Ernst Toller and Lilo Linke but other obvious escapers from Germany.

Apart from political get-togethers or angry arguments, which might get somewhat out of hand, I'm inclined to think that there was considerable emotional build-up at these parties. Nowadays the main age for interesting sexual encounters has shifted downward into the teens. With us it was later. We had time and energy, and it made the parties more stimulating and entertaining for others, though there may also have been painful encounters. The children knew vaguely that there were grown-up goings-on of some kind; I don't think this worried them, but was an extra interest. Sometimes, I'm sure, they took sides, at least among themselves.

In general there was very little drunkenness at the parties, and as far as I noticed, very little serious necking, though couples might wander off into the garden on a summer evening. In the whole time there is only one mention in the Green Book of a cocktail party. That would certainly have been more expensive on drinks that our usual informal big party starting around nine. Sometimes there is an excuse, someone's birthday, Guy Fawkes or Midsummer Eve. In the first ten years or so we did acting games at parties; sometimes we danced, and once I remember we put on a show called *Daisy and the Sheik*. The main performer in this was the nursery rocking horse in different caparisons, with me as Daisy being carried off by sheik after sheik. We didn't take sheiks seriously in those days!

Preparations for the parties were always rather fun. I shopped around, coming back with white cardboard boxes of *petits fours* or macaroons or fruit pâté from the Army & Navy made into coloured loops. The children helped to put these things out on to silver or china, no doubt snatching a few cakes which didn't worry me so long as it was in reason; I had done the same myself. They took things round during the party. We probably had bowls of fruit salad and cream or trifle, hot cheese straws and little fresh cakes made by the cook. There would certainly have been sandwiches cut thinly from fresh bread. Dick would have opened bottles of red and white wine with perhaps a punch or fruit cup. I remember once making Athole brose and thinking how good for one's skin the steeped oatmeal must be. There might possibly be cider, but no beer, and little in the way of spirits, at any rate at first, and very likely coffee halfway through. Parties were usually over by midnight.

Sunday suppers became more usual when the boys were back from school and wanted to have their friends in. They were always informal and rather nice. They were often in the garden and if it was cook's Sunday out I would make an enormous omelette and a bowl of salad.

A comparatively formal black-tie dinner party took more organising, especially if somebody cried off without giving one enough notice and one had to hunt round to make up numbers. Single men were always so much in demand that they were hard to get, but it was essential to have equal numbers of men and women. Six or ten were good numbers, as then Dick and I could be at opposite ends of the table. Eight or twelve were harder to control. Usually there was some purpose for the party and the seating had to be organised so that those who had been specially invited together could sit next to one another or possibly be able to talk across me, in which case my job was to bring them both into the conversation without leaving out the two ladies beyond. Dick and I would discuss this carefully beforehand and if it was a large party I would write and put out place cards.

At a formal dinner party ladies were taken in to dinner on their dinner partner's left arm. If one was dining out and there were new faces, one often set one's fancy on someone but then was allotted to someone else; it couldn't be helped. Each person talked to his left-side partner and then after the main course turned to the other side for perhaps quite a different conversation. Still, there could be a change after dinner, and the pattern was slowly breaking down. Dick and I both had to be prepared to talk to people two or three places off if there appeared to be any social difficulty. At the same time we must see that people were getting properly fed and possibly had the chance of a second helping, and that by the end, each guest had got his chance of meeting those he really wanted to talk with. At a big party there was more of this to do, including remembering names, as well as watching to see that the shy or less attractive had friends and food provided for them.

At the end we would pass round fruit and sweets ourselves and finally I would catch the eye of the lady on Dick's left and we would sweep out in our nice evening dresses. The convention was that the men could take an extra half-hour over their glasses of port or Madeira, in revenge for which their coffee was apt to be tepid while the ladies got it hot. The men were supposed to be talking about money while we talked about sex. It wasn't a bad, or indeed an anti-feminist arrangement, and gave the females a chance of going to the loo in peace.

In the later Thirties Dick started bringing in spirits of some kind around eleven in the evening—probably whisky and brandy, but always home-made lemonade as well. I don't think people worried very much yet about having a drink before driving, for the roads were so much safer and less crowded, and neither we nor our guests ever had any after-dinner accidents.

LOVELY ABROAD

WHILE I WAS writing *The Conquered* and *When the Bough Breaks* I was passionately eager to see the actual places, Gergovia and Alesia, to touch the stones, to feel the same sun and wind. So my brother and I went walking in the Auvergne, staying in *estaminets* were I was always bitten by fleas; he, unfairly, never. It was very hot. On those mountains covered with blaeberries three times the size and juiciness of Perthshire ones, I took off my thick tweed skirt and walked in black silk knickers which were normal hot-weather wear, quickly slinging on the skirt again if we met anyone, which we seldom did. Once we came down hungry to a village, ate well, washed it down with red wine and staggered into an old quarry full of wildflowers to sleep it off. And turned dizzily towards one another. And suddenly Jack was shocked to his respectable Haldane soul. I wasn't. But that was all. The next year he had gone to Cambridge.

Dick and I went to Vézelay and Chartres and to Lascaux when the caves were still open and the impact tremendously strong. Then there was north Italy, Ravenna where I was deeply moved by Byzantine murals and Galla Placidia on the edge of two cultures, poor dear. There was always the gorgeous foreign food, fried squid and *gelati* in Venice, apricot ices in thick china cups in Cracow, grapes, peaches and figs, or perhaps some new wild berry that was interesting if not delicious. Above all there was the widening of the imagination through sight and hearing. Dick liked to take his time ordering meals and the wine to go with them. I found this rather boring, but all the time there were the stories and poems going about in my head and picking up fragments from all around, and I usually had a very small notebook in which I could write inconspicuously if we were sitting in a café.

Later on, in the Thirties, Italy became less pleasant. We knew better than to tangle openly with the *fascisti*, but there were some faintly nasty occasions. Once, too, we walked through the Black Forest, and then did some sight-seeing in Dresden and Nuremberg, enough to make us feel very unhappy when they were bombed to bits.

Once Dick, Jack and I, all three of us, went over from Marseilles in a cattle boat to Tunisia, then a kind of extension of France—at least to us. We started playing hide-and-seek and I hid among the tethered cattle; they couldn't find me and got quite frightened. We went south to Kairouan and Sbeitla and discussed the fall of Rome and rise of Islam with considerable academic knowledge but, I am sure, without relating it at all to the state of the country or its people. Today, none of us could afford that neglect.

We needed no passports for nearer European countries; our British presence was enough—or even too much. But beyond the usual bounds we had passports that unfolded like Britannia's mantle. There was a square somewhere—Prague, was it?—high, romantic frontages, a crowd of foreigners shouting something incomprehensible and suddenly at the far side the sound of shooting. Dick quickly wrapped the passport round me. Naturally, all was well. Only foreigners got shot.

I went by myself to Oslo, one early spring, deep snow still. I ought to have learned to ski, but there were no ski schools at that time. Instead I went to museums and wrote and looked and looked again at the Viking ships until I felt I held them in my mind. I was suffering from emotional wounds and had to get rid of them. So I went on to Sweden and walked for whole days on roads between snowbanks and called on Selma Lägerlof whose books I had enjoyed so much. She had a beautiful wreath of evergreens on her door and must have been rather surprised at her walking admirer with thick shoes and rucksack. Over in Gotland I walked again, further than I would have if I had realised that the milestones were in the old Swedish measure, so that my disappointing three-mile walk along the cold sea edge under the strange ancient fortifications was really fifteen English miles. I knew very little Swedish beyond Yes, please, so when I got to an inn I always seemed to get an egg and a glass of milk.

Later Dick and I went to Stockholm, where the modern architecture bowled us over, but still more, seeing Karl Milles and his garden of sculpture. If one was not there at the exact hour, the door did not open, but we, for once, were punctual. The buildings and fountains, though no longer so astonishingly new, are still very fine, though the Town Hall murals, when I saw them twenty years later, had dated. But Milles has, I believe, achieved a degree of immortality, this blue-eyed, delicate-looking man standing by a lovely bowl of snakes'-head fritillaries, working only on the hardest possible stone.

But to get the real flavour of between-war travel, I go back to 1924, the year when Dick's parents stood us a hired car in Vienna. We had gone there via Salzburg, Innsbruck and Linz. We swam in the ice-cold, grey-green Danube, where, doing one's best, one could just keep steady against the current; here a large fish nosed me and bounced away. In the hired car, with Franz, the Swiss driver, we went into Hungary and eventually—after hectic negotiations with the Czech officials over taking the car across the border—on into Czechoslovakia. I have kept an account written at the time which renders in serio-comic detail the night and day we spent at that frontier post, plied with quantities of Tokay by the kindly Hungarian guards who gave us shelter while we waited to load the car on a train, the only way the Czechs would allow us to take it into their country.

In the end we got through into Czechoslovakia, where on Sundays the peasant women still wore splendid embroidered skirts, aprons and beribboned caps. In the high Tatras the gophers sat on their behinds beside their holes staring at us, and there was a whole new flora to collect and draw. And at Brno I found the statue of Mendel in a rather dull square with a plain red church. We went to the flower market—always such a pleasure in a foreign city—and I bought a bunch of mixed carnations, colours and stripes, which I felt would appeal to the ghost of the great geneticist and I laid them at his stone feet.

Family holidays started in France, first at Varengeville, a small village on the top of the cliffs, a few miles west of Dieppe. These were joint holidays; the families with children lived in fairly basic chalets, eating at the hotel, which was no doubt far from *luxe* by modern standards, but fine for us. We went down a steep path to the sand and rather chilly swimming, and tremendously enjoyed one another's company, playing all kinds of games in the evening, especially the wine glass game where, preferably by candlelight, an up-ended wine glass is made to slide over a table, spelling out words from a laid-out alphabet in answer to questions. This always became very lively when my brother and I were playing. A certain modicum of belief is helpful in this game, and also a verbal ingenuity in realising what the first few letters of a word may be pointing to, and then helping it. We also played Halma and chess, including four-handed or blind chess, but none of these modern board games, where the first day is taken up with studying the rules. We were all under thirty and the children small enough to go to bed early, sandy feet and all. It was here and much to the pleasure of the hotel that I was awarded the Palmes de L'Académie Française, my only official recognition from anywhere, for *The Conquered* and their own Vercingetorix.

There are browning and fading photographs of us all: the Spring Rice family, Diarmid Coffey from Dublin, Karin Stephen from Bloomsbury, Eileen Power, most delightful of mediaeval historians, my brother, Theodore Wade Gery from Wadham, Professor Meredith of Belfast University, a great friend, Liz Belloc and half a dozen others. Once Stella Benson, back from China, was a visitor. Even my mother came. Folkestone to Dieppe was a pleasant sea passage and we used to go to Dieppe, in those days a pretty, very definitely French little town, to meet the boat and buy extra fruit and cakes. Customs formalities were minimal and we could park anywhere.

Further along the coast was Deauville, where my cousin Margaret, now married to her second husband, the impressionist painter, Paul Maze, was staying with her family. It was a lot smarter; we could observe the current French fashions. Paul dashed off enchanting water colours of the beach, the striped umbrellas, the bathers lying around the line of the bright sea. Margaret's daughter, Pete, much influenced by her step-father and the impressionist circle, was also beginning to paint very promisingly.

There were also family-and-friends holidays in England; we went to Port Meirion, the Williams-Ellis fantasy hotel, not yet finished nor as expensive as it was to become later. It had a great, romantic wild garden and beyond this again the slate quarries which Agnes Miller Parker, our Hammersmith neighbour, painted so often.

Then in 1927, we went to Athens and the Greek islands, again with a few friends, including Margery Spring Rice, Theodore Wade Gery and Liz Belloc. It had been arranged before and the others urged us to come, partly to get us out of our misery about Geoff.

> But listen to the wind, you said
> Listen to the wind in the rigging
> Small waves on the counter jigging,
> Listen to the wind in the rigging
> And forget about the dead.

We hired a yacht, partly crewing it ourselves, with a totally inadequate auxiliary engine and an equally inadequate captain—he was always in trouble over clearing his papers and on one island all of us were temporarily arrested coming out of the sea in swimsuits, presumably by the local Turkish officials. But at that time it was still clear that Britons never never never would be slaves or even put under arrest by lesser breeds, so we were not much bothered. The islands had not yet been archaeologically organised for tourism or even completely noted by the archaeologists. Wade Gery found a new inscription on Thera. Here the volcanic plug bubbled with hot sulphurous springs and the sea swam with strange floating pebbles of pumice that knocked against the sides of the boat all night as we slept on deck.

The swimming was wonderful. We ran out of food before Aegina and I swam ashore (I was in my second month of pregnancy and very hungry) and swam back with long bunches of grapes and dark bread, too hard to spoil with spots of salt water, over my shoulders. My hair was still long and got full of sparkles out of that phosphorescent sea. Whenever we landed friendly people came and asked where we were going and what relations we all were to one another. At Delphi there were nightingales singing in a dark thick bush, but lazily. We threw stones into it to make them go on singing. Those red echoing clefted cliffs. But no oracle spoke to me.

Some years later I went to Greece again on a Hellenic cruise of some kind; it meant I could take the boys cheap as well as myself in return for lecturing. But the food was awful and they only let me lecture to the second class as I had no proper academic qualifications, or perhaps because I made up so much of it, since I was quite clear that I knew what it must have been like then and this was what I described to people.

At some point in the early Thirties I had been, or imagined myself to be, rather unwell. I went to some kind of quack doctor pressed on me, as I recollect, by our good friend Noel Brailsford. I think he was a Viennese and he professed to find dire symptoms, but at any rate said that I needed a change. So Agnes Miller Parker and I went off to the Canaries in a Norwegian cargo boat that took a few passengers. It was very rough crossing the Bay and we slid up and down in our bunks or held on to any railings, occasionally encouraging the first mate's ten-year-old who was rather frightened. Unlike the other passengers we duly turned up at every meal with a good appetite for salt pork and beans. The Captain beamed at us: 'I lose money on youse girls!' Agnes did some lovely sketches of our adventures. I wrote.

We had a nice time in the Canaries, and swam from a splendid empty beach full of enormous waves which, we found out later, was forbidden as too dangerous. Agnes had to go back but I was going on to Morocco and there was a Spanish cargo boat which took occasional passengers. As soon as we sailed it became clear that the ship's officers looked on me as prey, but I found a protector in a Jugoslav Communist seaman, with whom I swapped Marxiana. There was also a family of Portuguese acrobats who charmingly taught me to walk barefoot along a spar. I had a fair amount of adventures in Morocco and spent very little money, but the constant male-dodging and pushing wardrobes in front of doors was rather a bore. French lorry-drivers in a Moslem atmosphere are not exactly my cup of tea. I got to Gibraltar and came back steerage in a P & O which would have been unpleasant but that I found friends coming back from India much more comfortably and spent the days with them. I had met a few politicians, including the infinitely charming Lyautey, but felt—unusually for me—that I didn't know nearly enough about the situation even to write an article!

It was in the mid-Thirties that we went to Zarauz, a seaside resort in northern Spain, with a formidable sea current. I was caught in it and pulled out to sea but managed to fight my way back and not tell anyone. Another British tourist was drowned. Here one evening we found a long line of men and women making patterns of dancing through the half-lit streets. The others were not interested, but the hotel waiters and chambermaids took me with them into the dance, where I happily missed hours of intellectual discussion by the others. At Zarauz there were *churros*, a kind of light doughnut affair, in all the cafés and there was a *churro*-eating competition which Denny won easily. Val, by then four years old, had trouble with the customs on the way back, as they thought her doll was being used for drug smuggling and seized it. Luckily Nurse intervened. By this time we were no longer sharing with the Spring Rice family but with the Coles and their circle.

The next year we went to Madeira by boat, to a hotel on the high cliff; in those days transport was by an ox-drawn sledge up steep paved lanes between high hedges, and great fun it was. Avrion at seven was busy exploring the hotel back garden, probably more interesting at his height than for those older who would have missed some of the most curious leaves, roots, slugs and what-have-you. Below the hotel was a swimming pool and beyond that a rocky islet we could get out to, where Lois, then nine years old, was washed off into the sea by a huge wave, but could swim and was rescued. But it is still an awful moment to remember. Her long black hair was hot and a nuisance and I persuaded her to have it cut if I had mine cut at the same time, so we both came back bobbed. I still wear the almost indestructible flower-woman's striped skirt which I bought there.

PATTERNS OF LOVING

SOCIAL PATTERNS USUALLY get changed by technological progress—here by effective contraception, which was itself part of women's emancipation. Of course it was not the only thing, but it was probably the main reason why the accepted ideas and practice of marriage and of extra-marital relationships altered so much between 1920 and 1940. The other reason was in the general status of women, their newly independent feeling after the war years and the realisation that women could do all the men's jobs as well as their own and were just as capable of making important decisions. More had gone into the professions with the sense of freedom that paid work gives.

Dick and I were in the middle of all that. When we married in 1916, Dick on a week's leave from the war in Flanders, we were 'in love' but had astonishingly little idea of what that meant in marital practice. We were both virgins, but you must remember that at this period that was not unusual for a young man in his early twenties. Dick had asked the regimental doctor if there was anything he ought to know and the doctor had answered that he would soon find out for himself. Not unnaturally we did not do very well by one another. This went on after he came back, first on sick leave recovering from a fractured skull and a few minor injuries, then on an army course. I got little or no pleasure, except for the touch of a loved body and the knowledge that for a time he was out of the front line. The final act left me on edge and uncomfortable. Why was it so unlike Swinburne? Where were the raptures and roses? Was it going to be like this all my life? I began to run a temperature.

Dick went back, now on the staff. I had my baby. Then I heard about and bought Marie Stopes's *Married Love*, rushed out, bought a second copy and sent it off to Dick. It seems incredible now that this book was such an eye-opener. Why had none of these elementary techniques occurred to either of us before? Well, they hadn't. It was not the kind of thing young people talked about or, in spite of the poets, thought about.

So far so good. A marked increase of happiness. I stopped running a temperature. But some damage had been done. We were both, so to speak, open to something better. If I left out what happened after some twelve years of marriage, the record would not be true. For most of my life my love relationships affected my writing. Presumably this is true for everyone in the arts; we swim much more in the emotions. In order to observe we have to be thin-skinned, easy to hurt, and perhaps we observe too much for comfort. I cannot be sure that from this distance I am writing with any accuracy, and in a sense none of this matters now. But it mattered deeply to me then: the shape of a hand, the tone of a voice, the writing on the letter that came two posts late.

How then did things work out? I cannot but ask the young woman who was myself half a century ago if it was as important as all that, this state of being in love, this entanglement of bodies? Did it not interfere with other relevant activities, destabilising the mind which should be on the job? But she would answer yes, it is utterly important, it is fuel for the imagination, it puts brilliance and vigour into one's vision. More, it is mutual kindness, tenderness, it is a nest against chaos in the middle of a tossing tree. These are only images. The truth of love is not in words. And anyhow, she would say, this is something I intend to have, so stop arguing! Yet looking back on it now, I remember the pain almost more clearly than the delight, whereas with the relationships which did not include love-making—for instance with Lewis Gielgud or Angela Blakeney Booth or Aldous or Zita Baker, the only remembered pain is at their death.

I did not take a lover until such time as Dick too was looking elsewhere; this timing is important and means that there is less likelihood of hurting the other partner. Unhappily it is rather unlikely in practice to work out like that, and there is always the possibility that the one of a couple who is left out of a budding new relationship may start an unsatisfactory and really unwanted external love affair just so as to make things seem all right.

Perhaps Dick and I were lucky. We both got something which neither was able to provide for the other. Being married is a value; it is bread and butter; but it may make one less able to provide the cake. Several of our friends were, like us, behaving in ways which I think would have been utterly unacceptable even twenty years before. But we were far from being casually promiscuous; we thought ahead; married people in the professional classes were on the whole very anxious not to endanger a good relationship with spouse or children.

Dick and I had earlier agreed to be truthful with one another; perhaps we were too truthful, since it is the minor details which hurt. We had both decided rationally that we were not going to be jealous, since this is a very degrading emotion which should not be allowed to take possession. Both felt it sometimes, but on the whole managed to keep it in check and not say or do anything too hurtful. Certainly we were both a little hurt from time to time but never unbearably, never so that it interfered with our family life.

I think each of us realised that the other needed new channels of communication to other lives, other ideas. Perhaps too we needed the touch of a stranger, the exploration of another mind and another body. This mattered to me over my writing, to Dick over his political and perhaps his social life as well. One may be able to get this communication in other ways, for instance through shared and intense religious or political experience; but it is quicker in bed, sometimes even too much of a short cut. Yet I still believe that this did not spoil our basic relationship with one another, our deep affection, respect and loyalty, even when the other partner was doing something very much out of the pattern. And I went on getting worried if for instance Dick went off fishing or shooting alone and was late getting back. Later, as I shall try to show, I shared his political life as well as I could.

The love and the communication of ideas which mattered most to me came gradually, after many years of friendship and working together, increasingly delightful but then turning, as we should have foreseen, into stress and tension. And then—? Perhaps this summarises it:

But after all and after all and after all,
Was this all we wanted?
Through the green-tented, still air, scented,
From the great height of the lime tree small pale petals fall.
Was this, then, all?

Where's wrong, how wrong, to whom wrong?
After that forsaking, those aching years of avoiding seeking,
It is as if I had known all this, all, all along,
And the Oxford bells going ding dong, ding dong.

For indeed it is all, but not all. So in the end for a few years he and I were occasional lovers, snatching an afternoon or evening, usually out of doors; I remember snow drifting down through bare branches, melting on our warm skins. Cows quietly watching us like gods through the river mist, us lying ground-low in their field, a place beyond space, beyond time. Yet I remember equally the earlier times, before the stress of should we, shouldn't we, wandering and talking in Kew Gardens, as so many other couples have done, each thinking this is our special tree under which once you said—I said—or walking through the Quantocks, the crying of lambs as we came down from the tops into the deep soft combes. Sunshine in woodland coming suddenly lights up, changes colour, reveals shape, raises our spirits with beauty: so with love.

Clearly among youngish people meeting together the look, the spark of sex will fly. Normally one follows it up a certain way, then decides against going on; it has turned out not to be important or it could hurt somebody else. But sometimes there is no just impediment. I had the feeling at the back of my mind that Midsummer Eve did not count; no guilt could be attached to anything that happened then. I think this was a good idea and something of the kind might be socially helpful, but perhaps the sense of the seasons has left too many town dwellers for such things to work out. Occasionally I had someone after me whom I did not want, but it was embarrassing to say no and I tended to leave it almost—but not quite—too late. Once or twice I scrambled out of a situation with a certain lack of face.

Part of what I got and I believe gave was encouragement in what was being thought about and done, at a fairly difficult period of social mobility. Several of my friends, including my husband's first love, were in the same kind of position, feeling that there was something missing from their marriage but not wanting to break it up, wanting quite genuinely to help it. Dick's lover, like me, had young children whom she did not want to upset. Yet I think that, although we pretended otherwise, we and such of our friends as were living in the same way felt a certain degree of moral guilt. Or again—were we absolutely certain about our contraceptives? As it happened I only know of two failures among all my friends. But how could we avoid the feeling of slight guilt after our upbringing? Perhaps Dick felt it less. I sometimes hoped I was fighting for more freedom, for a whole generation of women. My daughters perhaps? Who, I dreamed, would be able to have children by several chosen fathers, uncensured. That was the kind of dream many of us had. But I at least sometimes felt morally uneasy waiting for the big stick.

I had other loves besides the one who meant most; they overlapped the deep heart-ache which for me went on long after that man and I had agreed to part, when I was fairly certain I would never see him again and yet longed to. But that heavy, unseen, powerful current went to turn the mills of work and imagination and I believe those two or three others who were in love with me even for a short time were taken into states of intenser living and I think delight; I gave as good as I got.

If I re-read the books which I wrote at that time I can tell who was occupying some other part of my mind, occasionally interrupting:

> Expecting the telephone,
> The papers slide on my table.
> The thought that should square them has flown
> From a quivering impulse
> And a mind unstable.

The keys of my typewriter
Go dead. The tension in the writing
Checks and twists tighter
Between the woman in the cave
And the two men fighting.

Pen stabs on blotting paper,
No words come through
As my people dim and taper,
Only the cold, enforced, unwanted
Image of you.

But the writing went on in spite of these interruptions which, after all, were my own doing and which, as I well knew, sharpened and intensified all my abilities. For that alone I miss them now.

Looking back, there appears now to have been ample time for all these emotions to take their course, to be reconsidered, above all to be talked out among ourselves and our friends in what appears in retrospect to be a long and tedious way. But by now I have rather forgotten how entrancing to any generation one's coevals' experiences are. I was never one to keep my pleasures to myself. Or my poems. But what are love poems for? Letters which I kept for their sweetness are now dry brown comb, the honey hardened away and gone.

Yet when I think back to those I loved it is not only the ones I went to bed with who matter. There was Lewis Gielgud with whom I wrote all those plays, to whom I rushed across from London to Paris. We were as close as two friends could possibly be, picking up from one another at a glance before the words were out of our mouths. I asked him once why he had never made a pass at me and he said: 'Oh, I suppose the old school tie and all that.' He was another old Etonian though it sat lightly on him. But I suspect it was that our relationship as friends and collaborators was so satisfactory, delightful and perennially amusing, though we discussed seriously many serious matters, that anything added would have been too much.

And Aldous, who was like another gentler brother? He was clearly no monogamist but I expect the brother–sister relationship was too strong. Nor would I have had for him the interest of the unknown and unexplored. Once during my engagement to Dick he asked me to explain exactly what it was like being in love. I couldn't. Useless! And Gervas, the other Huxley cousin and member of our gang? But again we were perhaps too close to start with.

Liz Belloc was part of our life, both at Cheyne Walk and at River Court or in Sussex running the house for her father, when Dick and I went down to stay with Hilaire Belloc at the Mill. There was French cooking, wine, lovely salad and Liz fussing over the olive oil which must be the best. Hilaire sang to us the Shanty of the Nona, the Owers Light, the Delicate Flower. On Sunday mornings the Bellocs went off to Mass. Dick and I slept in. We all had a big late breakfast and played road hockey while the Church of England were going to their service. Later in my life I wouldn't have done that, since no doubt people's feelings were hurt and their convictions remained unchanged. But it was a ploy like not standing up for *God Save the King*. Liz and I both wrote poems in the Mill and some of my stories were written there. Sometimes we wrote the poems to one another.

Liz came with us on several holidays, and always she went dashing off by herself to wild places. She wasn't strong but didn't let that interfere. Someone at the Foreign Office rang me up to say that she was ill, probably with pneumonia, somewhere in the high Andes—could I contact the Belloc family? I tried but couldn't, nobody answered the phone. What was I to do? Finally I marched off to Westminster Cathedral and told them, no doubt rather aggressively, that I wanted someone prayed for and would pay for it—I had no idea if this was correct. But when I told them who it was they couldn't have been more amiable. All would be organised immediately and no question of money. Liz recovered and the family were grateful.

But we had a quarrel about religion, I can't in the least remember what or how or why, but we were both obstinate and then suddenly we were rolling on the floor like two dogs biting one another. She went away and never came back. I kept thinking, Oh, she's sure to turn up. But the months and years went by and there was an edge of increasing sadness and loss and finally giving up hope. Her reason, I think, comes into one of her published poems. Only once she wrote to me after my brother died in India and I wrote back long and loving, hoping so much to see her again. But there was never anything more. Could we have borne to see one another old?

Back beyond her was Angela Blakeney Booth. We met at Lady Courtney's house at one of the Women's International League meetings. I put her at once, gorgeous red hair and all, into *The Conquered* and called her Coisha. We were devoted friends for many years until her death in the Sixties, though we went very different ways. Her mother's house in the Isle of Wight comes into *We Have Been Warned* as Helm; one evening I saw a Hobyah-type fairy there. Angela and I sympathised with one another's love or hate affairs and shared idealistic political views. I read her my poems, lots of them, and she responded as only one under-thirty can to another. It is so curious that we no longer ring one another up, write long letters, arrange to meet, have this constant mutual awareness which is friendship. The page turns and suddenly there is nothing.

I can't not remember Llewelyn Powys, the first time, driving with beautiful Isobel, his niece, behind the clopping horse through winding roads to the windy house, high up, and then the talk, cautious at first, then easy and warm, reaching out tentacles towards further closeness. For a few years I saw a lot of Lulu; together we watched the fox family in the undercliff below the chalk and smelt sun-soaked whin and sea spray. I wish now I had made love with him, as he wanted, but somehow it didn't work in my own life. And then he died.

When I write about my old friends, still more when I read their letters, it is difficult to remember that they are no longer alive and close. It is perhaps hardest with my brother. After the rather overpublicised divorce in which he was co-respondent, he won his case against the academic Sexviri—do they any longer exist?—who had demanded that he no longer sully the halls of Cambridge

(Professor Hopkins and I were both called as character witnesses). He married in 1926. At first things went fairly well; I tried very hard to be pleasant and my parents made great efforts. But after a visit when I was desperately unhappy after Geoff's death, in which I not only got no sympathy or affection but painful accusations, I came near to killing myself. The black shutter came down for the first and I hope the last time. After that I saw little of either Jack or his wife Charlotte. Things went badly between me and Prof (as he now liked to be called) in the Thirties, though we did write to one another, usually showing off and sending each other our own books. Nor did it come totally right until many years later when Helen, his second wife, a lot younger than both of us, with great courage knocked our stupid heads together and restored some of what had been lost.

Yet there were breaks in this and our war never included Dick or the children. In the middle of a bad phase Jack came over and read some of his splendid Dr Leakey stories aloud to Lois. He wanted desperately to have children himself; perhaps a bad attack of mumps when he was a boy had stopped that. I think he could hardly bear it sometimes when it was I who had the children. He had to take it out on me.

But plenty of my old friends are still around. There is Sonja Meyer with whom in the hard late autumn of 1944—the first moment I could get back to Denmark—I tried to walk across the broken piled ice of the Sound to buy sweets in Sweden. After a mile or two we turned back, beaten but laughing and together again, as we have been ever since. There is Gertrude Hermes who once had a commission to make some fairly pornographic engravings. She consulted me; luckily I had some classical erotica. But how exactly did these people in the black figure vase paintings go about it? We got down on the floor. 'No, you put your leg *there*. Ooh, it's too uncomfortable! Might be easier in bed. No, you ought to be the other way up, let's look at the photo of the vase. I suppose a Kalokagathos practising at the gymnasium every day might have had the right muscles. Not me. I wonder they didn't get dislocated!' This resulted in a set of charming little pictures and the characters appear to be enjoying themselves whichever way up they are.

There was a younger generation whom I got to know, mainly through my cousin Christine Willans, who was living with us at River Court while she worked in London. One of them was a fellow student of hers from Lady Margaret Hall: Elizabeth Harman, strikingly pretty and intelligent with Chamberlain blood on her mother's side. I felt certain she would get whatever she wanted, probably in politics. My match-making tendencies were aroused. I couldn't help feeling how well assorted Elizabeth would be with the equally bright young don Maurice Bowra. In 1929 we all went up to Cloan. I enjoyed being the temporary mistress, getting on well with the old domestic staff to whom I was still 'Miss Naomi'. Elizabeth and Maurice duly turned up by car and were met at the front door by Lois who walked out in a determined four-year-old way saying 'You go away and never come back!' They stayed, but the match-making didn't come off; Elizabeth married Frank Pakenham and Maurice sadly didn't marry anyone.

My necessarily sympathetic and matter-of-fact treatment of Hellenic love in my books put me in well with the highbrow homosexuals, who still at that time suffered from some legal and social troubles. Though certain aspects went easily: one great friend was given a Guardsman for his birthday—I was at the party—with no great expense involved, I gathered. My homosexual friends included revered seniors like Goldie Lowes Dickinson and Morgan Forster, but also Gerald Heard and beautiful Rudi Messel whom I met in the middle of the lily lake at Easton Lodge; we had both come there for a Fabian conference, but had temporarily dodged out of it to swim among the slithering, dangerous lily pads. I, or Dick and I together, would sometimes spend a few days with Rudi at Drewsteignton. I could always write there and then read aloud what I had written, always given love and encouragement. Once when I was in a post-miscarriage depression Dick packed me off there, and Rudi looked after me better than any woman would have. I got on well enough with his bucolic boyfriends. Once he asked me to tie and beat him, which I did, making fierce faces and quite enjoying it myself but not, I expect, hurting him as much as he might have preferred. Why should we insist on certain patterns of conduct?

Back in Hammersmith Gwen and Alan Herbert were good neighbours and Gwen painted well, but domestic problems seemed to turn up in the way they always do just when she was working best. Eric Kennington is out of fashion at the moment but I think his paintings will survive. I used to hang around his studio quite a bit trying to understand, as I did also with Wyndham Lewis, what makes people paint and how they go about transferring what they perceive into something which will give others the same sensations. Eric painted me at home in the house wearing a long white silk petticoat, leaning back with my hands clasped round one knee and my still-long hair loose. He did various studies of my hands and feet, not apparently put off by my thick ankles, then began the full-length picture in the studio. The only person I know who saw it was T. E. Lawrence, whom Eric also painted and who thought it good; but Dick didn't want it, was perhaps a little jealous, though Eric and I, fond enough of one another, had barely exchanged a friendly kiss. Perhaps feeling this, Eric cut the picture to bits, leaving only the head which Margie Spring Rice got and left to Val—but where has it got to now?

Most of our Hammersmith artist neighbours lived on a more impecunious scale than ourselves; among them were the MacCances. Mac himself was something of a phoney, demanding to be taken as a D. H. Lawrence-type genius; his wife, who in fact provided the family income and was a far better artist, was forced into practising mousemanship. We didn't even know she existed until months after he began coming to the house. Possibly this was partly the normal anti-feminism of the Scottish working-class man but there was a good deal of jealousy in it. However, as Agnes Miller Parker she did wood engravings, mainly illustrations for beautiful but expensive books, which are likely to survive anything her husband did.

Dick and I had not fully grasped this situation when we thought that we, the Spring Rice family and the MacCances should jointly own a cottage on Bledlow Ridge, a pleasant country drive in those days. It was called Pounds Scots, since Mac had suited himself into the character of a Scots nationalist with some wisps of Marx, and it really was a cottage, barely modernised, with interesting sloping ceilings on which the taller inhabitants bumped their heads, a wood fire constantly needing to be fed, a steep and narrow staircase and quite a squash when we were all there. Margery Spring Rice did most of the cooking; I was supposed to deal with the garden, but it was heavy clay over chalk and I just couldn't manage to make a decent job of it. There were of course no servants; it was assumed that the three women would do all the work while the men went for bracing intellectual walks. After a few years, that came to an end.

There were other painters and some writers in our lives at that time. Hammersmith was presumably thought in other circles to be very *avant-garde* and we had a good share of love and hate affairs, rushing in and out of one another's lives, having parties and from time to time swimming in the Thames which was surely much dirtier then than now. But it was fun to be swept up with the slightly buoyant tide past Chiswick Eyot, muddy to land on, across to the towpath and then the run downstream to a good starting point for getting back. It was thick brown water, stick- and bubble-streaked, but if we kept our mouths shut, not swallowing so much as a cigarette package or an old French letter, nothing went wrong.

There was also the Doves and a pub in Black Lion Lane where people played bowls. And there was an amiable confectioner and newspaper shop along at the end of Hammersmith Terrace where Lois and the Kennington boy attempted to disguise pennies as half-crowns with silver paper. The parents were discreetly told! All the people along the river had Boat Race parties and there was a cake shop that made us decorated Boat Race cakes. They also made a wedding cake for my cousin Christine when she married Michael Hope. My mother disapproved because he was 'in trade'—Hope's windows! But I approved strongly and the cake had pink windows opening on a foam of perilous seas in tossing white icing, and on the bottom layer the sweet Thames flowing softly. They were married at Marylebone Registry Office with Avrion and Valentine strewing the pavement with summer flowers.

There was always argument, admiration, dressing up and parties. Those at St Peter's Square were like today's: beer and bangers rather than claret cup and sandwiches as they would have been at more ordinary houses. Here were the poets and painters; here was Robert Graves, who might be delightful or might bite, according doubtless to his current relationship with the White Goddess. Here was Dylan Thomas holding forth, never sober. Here sometimes was Augustus John, who once suggested that as I had so many children I might have one by him. I felt this was an interesting party approach, but he had a glass of beer in each hand which inhibited the next step.

I don't think this kind of life has changed that much. People in the arts behave much as ever, with their furious jealousies and ganging up for and against one another. People feel insecure now. But by the mid-Thirties we too were beginning to feel increasingly insecure.

II

Portraits in Letters

INTRODUCTION

Over the years I have kept letters from all sorts of people, mostly literary or on the borders of politics and the academic world, because they were interesting or amusing letters or because I specially liked the people, but also because they were from men and women who seemed to me perhaps to matter not only to me but to my civilisation.

Sometimes I have found only one or two letters from people who I would have thought had written often. And again some letters are indiscreet, even now, and shouldn't see the light: letters it would be quite unfair to show to another person or to put into print. (In the letters quoted here I have occasionally excised names, or made small cuts for reasons of privacy or discretion.) Other letters are entirely personal or trivial, at least they are about what seem like trivialities now. Some are expressions of affection and interest which were very nice at the time but mean little today or which involve other people. I have bundles of family letters including dozens from my brother, yet I feel this is not quite the place for them. There are many letters from G.D.H. and Margaret Cole, from Margery Spring Rice and from Lewis Gielgud, but they would not help the outside reader to understand and visualise the period and the kinds of lives we led as I think the letters which I have chosen do.

Those who wrote these letters were all more or less professional writers even if they did other things as well, and a writer even scribbling something off or bashing a few lines on the typewriter is never so to speak naked. We are aware of an audience even if it never exists: an audience of one is as good as a million. I hope then that these letters I have put in will give a picture of the writers themselves and of the world in which they and I lived.

BEAUTY AND THE BICYCLE

FOR HOW MANY people is Professor Alexander of Manchester any more than someone whose books and lectures might be worth looking up if one is interested in, for example, the philosophy of aesthetics? Sammy Alexander and his bicycle that he sometimes caught his beard in? Or didn't he? Was this one of the many legends about him?

For my godfather was someone around whom legends grew. He came from Australia of all places and was consciously a Jew but cannot possibly have been at all orthodox. Anyhow I was not baptised; he was my adopted godfather. He had a gorgeous flowing brown beard latterly streaked with grey which meant that he never had to go to the trouble of buying, tying or wearing a tie. He was not well off but when he received a fee of £100 for a series of lectures he had the roof mended of the dingy little house in Withington he shared with his brother, but thought it would be a waste to get the bath repainted. When I was a child he turned up from time to time and brought me godfatherly small gifts, including things for my dolls' house. We had been corresponding since I was eleven or twelve—when I used to send him my poems. It was probably he who persuaded my mother to bring us up on Montefiore's *Bible for Home Reading*. But whatever he may have been religiously he had some fairly old-fashioned views of respectability, though not without the excuse of having been born in 1859. I have a letter written in 1916, just before my marriage, which goes:

> Though you are to be a war bride and married in a dirty registry office I am going to send you a little vase of William Burton's Lancaster ware to be put on a shelf or in a cupboard and to remind you that there is a mad old gentleman in Lancashire who rather likes you.

Now the reason for this is to be found in Aristotle's Ethics, Book 4, where he speaks of the virtue of magnificence; and any Oxford person like you must accept all he says as true. He speaks first of magnificence of expenditure on public occasions: 'But it may also be displayed on private occasions when they are such as occur but once in a man's life, e.g. a wedding or anything of that kind'. And it is not clear (though likely) that he is speaking only of the man's own wedding. Then afterwards he says 'Again the greatness of the result is not the same as the greatness of the expense; e.g. the most beautiful vase (or bottle) has magnificence as a present for a while though its price is something small and mean'. . . . So I am going to send you a little vase or bottle or pot on the authority of Aristotle. God bless you, my dear, and Dick.

He wrote to me while Dick was on leave after his broken skull; clearly he had been anxious and I had written to reassure him. He was at that time busy with the Gifford Lectures* which he was giving the next year; he had sent a draft of one of them to my father and goes on—but oh, dear, how illegible his writing is!—to say:

I am going to send your father a copy of the abstract of my Gifford Lectures which I begin on January 12th. I can't send you one because you will only detect some signs of insanity. As for the 'new realism' there's an American book of that name. Which is greatly read but we differ from one another—a very healthy sign. I wrote a paper called The Basis of Realism which possibly your father has not put behind the fire.

Clearly I had written to him about my serious reading for he goes on: 'I am glad you liked Weldon Kerr's book—it was very good I thought. You could find Bergson himself jolly reading—especially *Evolution Créatrice*. His last book is *Matter and Memory*, though it is also difficult.'

In the next letter at the end of 1917 he thanks me for

* *Space, Time and Deity* (1920).

photographs of myself and Dick and for my news of ourselves and Jack; he is so happy to hear I am going to have a baby. He is worrying about his lectures:

> I am trying to pull myself together for Glasgow where I go to lecture again from January off and on till February 18th. I expect the abstract reached your father—I daresay it is like ship's biscuit. Somehow I don't feel so energetic as last year but having to perform strings you up at the last moment. They were very good to me last year. Did you read Mr Pringle Patterson's book on the idea of God? I have just been reading a splendid book on Locke's theory of knowledge by Mr Gibson of Bangor.

The relationship by 1918 was fixed and durable. I am sure we corresponded a great deal and he would certainly have written me a charming letter after the birth of each of my babies. He felt very romantically about me and my children and kept quantities of photographs of us. He was deeply devoted to the idea of the family and ought to have been a father himself. But he supported all his own family and never had the chance to marry until it was too late; sometimes he spoke to me about that. Yet, with that perhaps conventional viewpoint, he was amazingly sympathetic with the affairs of the heart of those younger and sillier than himself; I told him a great deal about myself that I would not have told my parents or indeed anyone else of his generation. He took it all admirably lightly, and never gave the appearance of being shocked or even surprised.

I visited him at Withington. The first time, we travelled up together; he could always hear better in the train. But he was growing increasingly deaf and his bicycle was something of a Mancunian hazard. A well-wisher left him a few hundred pounds to spend on taxis, much to the delight of his adopted city. But did he ever take a taxi? Not at all. He continued with his dear bicycle, but I, for instance, when I went to stay, was advised to take 'one of my taxis'. At the door he hurried out, one hand in the trouser pocket which held the taxi money to pay the fare and give never more than threepence as a tip. I remember once surreptitiously adding to it when his back was turned. On money he had all the rather ridiculous Jewish characteristics, but laughed at them and himself. When we were together we almost always had one chat about money—how much we would get for articles, and so on, and he really enjoyed getting guineas instead of pounds! That didn't make him any the less generous, and I should think he gave away an astonishingly large percentage of his income. He was always ready to help refugees from fascism and his worries about them clouded the last years of his life.

In spite of his deep interest in aesthetics, there were few signs of external beauty in the house. His big study where we sat and talked about philosophy and books and life in general was deep in papers. Sometimes we walked in the streets of Withington. He knew about the people in the little shops and could tell me about progress in municipal housing. At that time Manchester weather seemed always to be grey, fogged over, a Lowry background.

The next letter I have found is much later on, dated November 1930. I had sent him some kind of an essay but what? It seems to have been about poetry, Eliot surely, perhaps Pound. No doubt it was also about beauty and this was something which interested my dear godfather very much and about which he was continually writing. I think sometimes he was really influenced by what I told him, for perhaps he did not get the same first-hand experience that I had. He writes—and his handwriting is getting worse!—

> I was vastly interested and I have copied into my notebook your account of the difference of poetry and prose to be cogitated upon. I don't find it as yet altogether satisfying. Your diagnosis of present poetry is very interesting to me as I don't really know the moderns. And you throw light for me on the meaning of Gerald Heard. As it happens when your paper came I had just read his book which you gave me at Christmas and I've not found energy till October to tackle. I thought it up to the last two chapters one of the most remarkable books I had read; but those two chapters baffled me and left me uncertain as to

> their meaning and their real reference in the preceding essay. I am told that he is now engaged on another book which will I hope present his view of the new stage more deeply and definitely. . . .

This shows, I think, how willing he was to accept merit in other, younger writers, and I believe he had correspondents all over the world. He was genuinely surprised when they treated him as a great man—which he was.

He goes on:

> The next time I am in London I must get out to see you and talk out this matter of poetry and prose and incidentally see the new Valentine. It's a relief to be writing to you. I've just come back from talking my stuff over the wireless. I think this whole thing is far too conciliatory in tone. There's no scientific disbeliever represented. I am told Malinowski was very good, but even he was an agnostic regretfully.

This is rather an interesting comment on the over-respectability of Reith's radio by somebody who was by no means a rebel but wanted to see all opinions represented which they certainly were not. They seldom are in a religious controversy. But this was part of his very real liberalism. He believed in freedom of thought and speech at all times. In the mid-Thirties he was very ready to work with left-wing organisations and did not fuss at all about being politically compromised. Incidentally he was charming to Dick who went up to Manchester to speak as a socialist.

My godfather did come and stay at River Court and I remember this well for he was going to some official dinner, a black-tie affair, and he carried only a small case when he arrived at our house. I asked if there was anything he would like to borrow for the occasion, but he said no, no, he was wearing his evening suit underneath. As it would have been quite out of context for his clothes ever to fit that was quite all right. But when he came back and after I had been up in his room to see that everything was as it should be, I asked again if he would like a pair of Dick's pyjamas. But again it appeared that his nightwear was already in place. Perhaps he just slept in vest and pants as indeed the majority in the British Isles did at this time.

When Walter Greenwood published *Love on the Dole*, in 1933, I reviewed it, praised it and went to see him and his sister at Salford. It seemed to me that any encouragement he could get would be very important for him at this time and I asked my godfather whether he would ask Walter and his sister Betty over to tea. Naturally he said he would be delighted and we fixed it up and then went out and bought quite a lot of iced cakes. Well, that was all right, but where were we to put them? Clearly tea would be in the big study but every chair was covered with papers or books. I suggested finally that we had better clear two or three chairs, for there would be several guests, one or two of whom might be very useful for Walter. The cakes could well be put on the top of piled papers which would act as little tables and so it was. Walter was shy, of course, but I think the whole thing worked out well and it was very typical of what I suppose was the Aristotelean view of magnificence that there were so many cakes! My godfather positively flirted with Walter's sister and often spoke of her afterwards, very warmly.

It was also about now that I went to a Manchester University function where he was presenting someone for a degree. At this time I was very much of a republican and dear Sammy was rather afraid that I would disgrace him by not standing up for *God Save the King*, which was played at some moment. I hadn't intended to embarrass him at all, but he couldn't be sure, so at the critical moment he turned round and shook his fist at me in the gallery! He trusted me over beauty, but not over politics.

The next letter was written in November 1933. It starts with an account of a visit to Oxford. My mother is 'cheerful enough and equal to the troop of visitors I found there—including a man whose car broke down on Sunday night whom they took in'. . . . 'The father seemed very fit and full of solutions.' At least I think that is the last word, but it might equally well be 'salvation'! But he keeps back the letter to put in a P.S. about my 'fairy tale', *The Fourth Pig*, which he had been reading:

> It seemed to me on first reading and now again on second reading that it ought to have been poetry. There is too much thought and passion in it for its present form. . . . You don't need me to tell you but the whole thing is difficult—as if I of all persons had a right to surprise you with that. Still I wish the poet had done it rather than the proseist. But it remains admirable and you will of course publish it.

Even when I was an established writer he was very fussy about grammar; he couldn't bear it if I wrote, to his mind, incorrectly. He was especially down on Scotticisms, which I used on purpose. But he saw the earliest manuscript version of my *Moral Basis of Politics*, encouraged me to go on and sometimes even marked the margin with an encouraging *Euge!*

There was always this feeling of warm affection in the letters. We really did act as godfather and god-daughter in a way that few people who have 'real' godparents do, but we chose one another late enough I think for each of us to know who the other was. It always remained that I was his cherished child and everything I did must have some kind of good purpose. I think also that he had great sympathy with women who were trying, as I was, to fend for themselves and their own art or profession in a man-made world. He understood what it was like to have the chains so recently taken from one's wrists.

And he always—as a godfather should—wanted me to be both good and happy. I have a letter of 1935 clearly about some memoir of my father which I was writing, in which my 'most affectionate S. Alexander' advises me to write nothing that 'your mother would disapprove or would hurt her feelings. You and she differ in principle on many things—don't exasperate the difference.' He goes on about our family relationships:

> Did I ever tell you how at a congress of philosophers at Reading —it was just after *Daedalus* was published—your father

(speaking in a discussion on heredity) referred to Jack's work and disavowed it both as science and philosophy but made it very clear to all of us how proud he was of Jack? I rather think he might think you went too far for him, but held his peace like a wise man and loved you not less.

Can you not take your material and recast it in the form of reminiscences? The memories you have of him and his manner of life and treatment of you, and if you refer to some of his opinions and the impression[?] that he might go the whole length of your way or indeed any part of it. Let it be just a picture and no *judgement*.

He was probably right. I was a lot too fond of making strict judgements, especially political ones and sticking by them irrationally in the way politicians tend to do.

Finally there is a letter of June 1937. It was the year before he died and he may have been feeling less strong but he was still as warm and outward-going. Clearly I had been writing in one of the periods of depression which most writers go through. He says: 'What are godfathers for if one can't blast one's sorrows to them and discharge one's spleen? This godfather thinks you are tired with nursing and the literary life and need a rest. But oh, don't consent to lose confidence in yourself—don't be like your godfather whatever happens. It will pass, accidie passes.' He then puts in a long quotation, from Goethe, I think, and goes on: 'I've been rejoicing in your (and Crossman's) *Socrates* all this afternoon. I could tell it was mostly you. I hear you talking and I like particularly the earlier pages where the poet speaks. I have fancied myself listening to a very wise child babbling to me and your dear presence has been by me in the room.' And then there is a square bracket and inside: ['But now speaks the godfather pedant: why didn't RHC keep you from these bits of quite unnecessary slovenly speech?] . . . Get well, dear old thing, and let the old godfather know—who by the bye (you may not know it) loves you quite a good deal. Ever, S. ALEXANDER'

ALDOUS BETWEEN THE WARS

I KEPT DOZENS of letters from Aldous. Why? Squirrelling I suppose. When I was asked to help with *Letters of Aldous Huxley** I found some of them but others turned up later. I wonder if he kept any of mine? If so they were burnt in the fire which destroyed his home while apparently he and his second wife, Laura, stood in a daze. With him, as with Wystan Auden, going to America and then the war was a break which was difficult to heal. No doubt we who stayed felt both pride and resentment; we were living real life, they were out of it. Both are rather nasty emotions.

Yet Aldous and I had been on affectionate terms over the between-war years. For me he was part of the family, a sort of brother, and when we met or telephoned or wrote short notes there was always family triviality, in-jokes and the short-cutting of people who know one another too well to bother to put it all down at length. And we could count on seeing each other from time to time in Oxford, especially in the immediately postwar days when some of our old friends who had been through it all and survived came back, tough and cheerful, seeing daylight again.

When Aldous married Maria Nys and a year later their son Matthew was born his material difficulties began to press on him, even though he was an immediate literary success. He wanted to live part of the time at least in London and asked all of us to look out for a flat. Clearly I got it wrong, from a postcard of March 1920 which says 'Thanks for the letter about house; but I don't know what you take us for if you think we can pay the best part of £200 a year rent—blooming Rothschilds'.

They were living at Forte dei Marmi at Lucca in the early Twenties, from which place I have a long letter:

* Edited by Grover Smith (London: Chatto & Windus, 1969).

Your letter provokes a tardy reprisal. But the writing of letters is one of the things I am not very good at. You knew it already perhaps? My excuses are better than usual: I am busy for half the day and I am idle during the other half. Obviously there is no available time in which to write letters. I am busy with a comic novel which I am pledged to finish in seven days' time—and which I shall not finish for another fifteen or twenty days. It is to be published in the Autumn I hope. Meanwhile I am grieved to hear of your unsuccess with your literary products. Your error is to write about Vercingetorix when you might write about me. What the public likes is not ancient Gaul but modern Gall (a ripe *paronomassia*). Gossip over 2,000 years old is apt to lose its spice. You should push on if not to modern times at least as far as the Renaissance. I have discovered the most superb historical character whose biography I propose to write some day—Paganini, the violinist: one of the real comics. He is the sort of man one should write historical novels about.

Why don't you come and spend a summer on this coast? It's perfect for children, it's not too hot if you lead a sensible life and go to sleep after lunch; it's extremely beautiful, a combination of sea, wooded plain and mountains and the present exchange is cheap. We calculate to be able to live in comfort on £300 a year here. The worst is however that I haven't got £300 a year—and I hesitate whether it is best to remain in Italy and risk not making the £300 out of the novel, stories or occasional journalism or whether it is wiser to come back to England to a certain £700 or £800 a year (on which one could live at about the same degree of comfort) to regular work and to fatigue. It's a problem. What a monstrous thing it is to have no money of one's own. In any case Maria and I will be returning in Oct.; perhaps for good, certainly for a month or two in order to find a new flat in which to put our furniture. You don't know of a convenient place of four or five rooms I suppose: not more than £100 a year? No—it isn't likely. We shall see you then I hope.

Above: The author on Aegina, about 1929

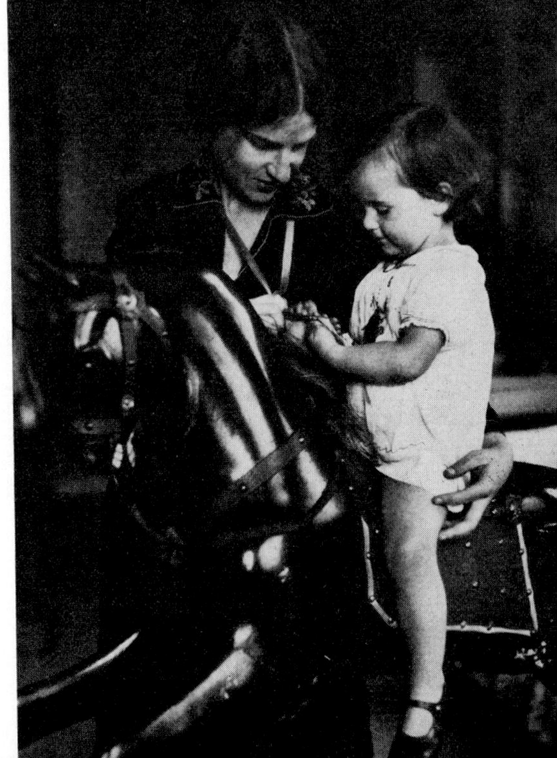

With Val in the mid-1930s

The Mitchison children, about 1930

Left : The author in the 1930s, in the headscarf in which Wyndham Lewis liked her to pose

Right : The young Wystan Auden

Murdoch about 1938

Val and Avrion with Tuppence the cat, Peter the rabbit, and Clym the Bedlington, about 1937

There is another letter, this time from Florence, thanking me for a letter and glad I liked 'the Leaves'* which, he now feels, are 'tremendously accomplished but in a queer way jejune and shallow and off the point. All I've written so far is off the point. And I've taken such enormous pains to get on it; that's the stupidity. All this fuss in the intellectual void; and meanwhile the other things go on in a quiet domestic way, quite undisturbed. I wish I could afford to stop writing for a bit.'

Clearly I had asked him if he had been reading about ethics, because he answers no, 'because it is perfectly obvious to me that ethics are transcendental and that any attempt to rationalise them is hopeless.' Then he goes on:

> You can discover the biological function of ethic, you can establish a connection between religion and intestinal stasis or sexual desires. But your discoveries will not in the least affect the value of the ethical and religious experiences of the individual. . . . On this subject Lao Tsze is most remarkable. His little book on the Tao is a sort of philosophical explanation of the ethics of Christianity. It gives the reasons why it is necessary to lose one's life in order to gain it: because it is impossible to have a real and absolute self so long as the superficial self is allowed to control things. . . . It is the same idea as lies at the bottom of the Yogi system. The same, of course, as in Christianity; but more explicitly and more intellectually stated.

He teases me again about not coming south: 'Your deplorable taste for the countries of the barbarians seems to keep you away from Italy. Which is a pity. If you bring with you a northern soul, northern friends and northern books, it is the perfect country. For you possess, indoors, the speciality of the north—the soul—and you have out of doors the speciality of the Mediterranean—beauty. In the north you have to be content with souls only.'

I wish he could have gone further north than the Midlands, or even Edinburgh, but I don't think he ever did. Only you have

* *These Barren Leaves* (1925).

to give the Highlands a chance; they may rain for a week—but then! This was something he never knew. It did mean I saw less of him for a few years, except for the occasional long letter. When he was in London it was likely that he was leading a rather sparkling life with friends in altogether other circles from mine. Who was I to penetrate?

Then they settled down at Sanary and I have several letters from there; clearly we are often in the middle of running political or social and literary arguments. One letter written just after Val was born goes:

> Lewis tells me of a daughter. This is to wish her all happiness and you too. There would be scope for a grand Ciceronian letter—Corinth on my left hand, something else on my right—but I lack the gift for that sort of thing.
>
> The summer is strange here as all over the world—occasional rain unprecedented for the time of year and when the sun shines, which it does like mad, I must say prodigious winds that never stop blowing either from the west or the east. Which is invigorating but rather annoying. We live picnic fashion without furniture while the workmen add on to and alter the house round us. It ought to be very nice when it's done but it takes the most devilish long time doing and I'm afraid we are in for another six weeks at least of tinkering. When we are installed I hope you will come and see us. It's a lovely part of the world. I've been writing some essays and have now got to begin meditating a novel. What a curious profession it is, this writing business and how lucky it is that the public doesn't wake up to the fact of our peculiar ridiculousness!
>
> Farewell dear Naomi.

Another from the next year goes:

> It was very nice of you to write so pleasantly of *Brave New World* and I am glad to think it amused you during your appendicitis. I am astonished that it has been taken so well as

it has been: I anticipated more outcry. So did Chatters—who made me cut one or two small things though very little. I hope you're getting over your appendix. These things take some time always I'm afraid. . . . Give my love to Gerald if you see him and tell him he said he'd write to me about that school in Devonshire—Dartington, isn't that the name?* Tell Dick I still think with amazement of the rum he gave me at the Athenaeum. Hail to thee blithe spirit rum thou never wast. . . . With my love.

We went to stay at Sanary. What fun it was! A lovely place; there was sun and fruit and coffee and lots of wild flowers. Dick was very much in his element, talking French which he always enjoyed both with Maria, who was of course completely bilingual, and with the various locals. He told me afterwards that Maria had explained to him exactly what was meant by high fashion and at last he understood what it was all about. This was followed up by a lunch with some very smart French neighbours and Maria afterwards telling us about high fashion modified for out of Paris! There was also a considerable amount of literary talk in French, mostly about authors whom I hadn't managed to understand. But I very much enjoyed going foraging with Maria. We got wild asparagus, very tasty, and baskets of snails which had to be starved before being eaten. Aldous protested mildly about this and much more when Maria and I found a scorpion in the garden and killed it. He was working probably on *Eyeless in Gaza* and one heard the typewriter if one cocked an ear. Maria protected him and cooked the snails.

Then again there was a gap. I saw him sometimes in London but we had gone in different directions. Only his white socks stayed the same, thanks no doubt to Maria. I was impressed by his pacifism but knew it was no use to me. Bad means alter good ends. Yes, but if good means are ineffective? One couldn't win.

* He must have been convinced by Gerald Heard, for Matthew went to Dartington. It was one of the schools I had looked at and turned down. I felt that if I was going to school myself it would be lovely but not what any of my children wanted and needed.

There is one other letter written from California in 1938, when war, or dictatorship, seemed to him to be looming:

> Thank you for your letter which I would have answered before but for an illness which laid me low for some weeks. I'm glad you liked the book* as well as you did. There are various things I would like to expand in it—e.g. the question of developing an economic and social technique of freedom and self-government which implies, I feel more and more certain, the revival by means of small power units and machinery of home and small shop production in scattered localities. . . . Meanwhile one has to ask oneself whether even an economically viable essay in anarchism has any chance in contemporary circumstances. It seems doubtful—as indeed does the possibility of doing anything satisfactory in these circumstances. It seems to me quite likely that we have reached a point where nothing we can do—from war to organised non-resistance—will be successful in getting us out of the mess. . . .
>
> Here I work at a novel, tried to sell a scenario I wrote this winter—without success since the films are in a state of nervous breakdown and panic—and see a certain number of scientists from the neighbouring seats of learning and one or two people connected with pictures (not many since most are really frightful and give one an awful feeling that one is insane when one is in their company). Lecturing up and down the country was fatiguing and generally a rather depressing process—though sometimes one ran into pleasant and intelligent people. Still there is a certain opacity about the human race that makes one wonder whether it is capable of running a society more complicated than this. This one's already a bit too much for us. Love to you both.

Well, there it is: the continuing affection. And perhaps that is the best that any of us can do for each other.

* *Ends and Means* (1937).

MORGAN COMES TO TEA

JUST BEFORE CHRISTMAS of 1923 I got a letter written on flimsy paper clearly torn from a pad, which thrilled me to the depths. I must have read it a dozen times for it was from someone I revered. It goes:

> Dear Madam,
> I venture to write you a line of thanks for *The Conquered.* I found it so moving and beautiful and the character of Meromic holding it together from first to last. It made me realise what life was—and is—of the half slave: the muddle of it, the ceaseless corrosion. I suppose we all view the past through our local interests and while reading your book I often thought of India and the Meromics I have seen there who suffer not of course with his intensity yet in the same way. The end seemed to me beyond all praise, the story of Esa re-entering so naturally but with the force of an evocation. Well, I wish there was somewhere to go to north or south but the sun of sorrow is all unrolled in vain so far as one can see and even if there was a place few of us are fit for the journey, it's more than a land that's missing.—I so much too admired the reserve that haunted all his human relationships; you made one feel that after Fiommar and his surrender he had lost the right to intimacy not merely the desire for it. Thanking you most sincerely, Yours faithfully, E. M. FORSTER

I wrote back falling over myself with pleasure, but I was at the same time writing an order for three or four shrubs from a nursery and out of excitement, I expect, transposed the letters. I haven't got his next letter but I remember that it sent back mine with one from him beginning 'Alas, alas, I have none of these nice things'. How does one remember the first line of a letter lost for fifty years? Well, it was burnt into me with my embarrassment though it seems rather a small thing to get into such a tizzy about.

But it was all smoothed over and after another letter from me and one from him saying, 'Do you care about meeting authors? I don't like it at all. . . ! . . . but might we meet sometime perhaps?', Morgan came to tea. He sat in the armchair on the right of the fireplace and I on a floor cushion, my favourite seat, looking up at him and feeding him with crumpets and chocolate cake. He put his cup down on the floor beside the chair, moved it a little and oh, dear, the cup was lost. We found it at once but his moment of embarrassment equalled mine about the shrubs. And we talked and talked about India, about books, about the world.

He came to tea the next year too. 'Not other people. If so it happened. I have nowhere nice to ask you to or I would.' I wrote to him about *A Passage to India*, and he wrote me about *Black Sparta* which he had been reading 'with the pleasure and pain with which I do read you'. He was blue-eyed and untidy, carrying things about that he might need, a book or an apple, and then forgetting where he had put them. His voice stumbled sometimes, tripping over a word. I became very fond of him.

Early in 1925 he writes:

> I have been busy or rather flustered for so long: it was because I was the latter that I couldn't come up to Crest House* that Sunday. I cannot abide a scramble. The result of this mental elegance will probably be that I shan't meet you yet a while for it is incredible that you should be free Friday afternoon or even get this letter in time to answer. However, I'll have a shot. We shall meet some time. I hope your work goes well. I have read your short stories of course since I wrote last. I look forward so much to the Aegospotami book; I hope you are fairly satisfied. Sometime I may show you my own one attempt at the historical in fiction: written long ago and turned down—about Gemistus Pletho and Sigismondo de Malatesta.

* The house of Sir Horace Plunkett, near Weybridge. Our friend Gerald Heard was at that time Sir Horace's secretary.

In another letter of 1925 he writes:

> Oh, possessions, possessions! We are bound to have them but why will we keep trying to include human beings among them? Ownership is after fear the wickedest thing in the universe; perhaps it's all the same thing, for we are generally afraid we may lose something. I wish I could have nothing and yet not be an ascetic. I believe you have the same wish and that is why your work is so sympathetic to me. I hope I haven't kept the MS too long. I have been away. I so enjoyed seeing you (did you know by the way that I called once, leaving a card all proper?). I will ring up or write again when I am in town.

I think this gives the feeling of the mutual build-up (for of course I wrote to him about his books just as he wrote to me about mine) of this period in the late Twenties and early Thirties. I am sure I needed it less than some of the others; I had lots of self-confidence, loads of energy; my neck of the woods was full of delightful nests and dens. But it was nice all the same to have the support when one felt a bit down.

The next letter is in 1929 and by this time, and just as well, Morgan is calling me dear Naomi: 'I am awfully interested in these two chapters and would like to read more now. Are you inclined to lend me some? Also do you like remarks to be made about a book while you are writing it or are you like me? Until the whole thing's finished I only want to hear from people that they want it finished—nothing more.' That would have been chapters of *The Corn King*. I had written to him about the general layout of the book and he puts in a P.S.: 'Trivial point—if you would care for an old temple for Ankhet's visit you can easily assume one to have survived from Rhakotis.'

He also writes in the same year (though I am not absolutely certain whether his dating of his own letters is really the actual date or what he thought it might be):

> I am sure these are the best short stories* you've done. Might

* *Barbarian Stories* (1929).

be the best anyone's done for a long time. The style has got so good. One of your problems in style happens to have been the same as mine and I see you solving it; the problem of realism without facetiousness. I shan't solve mine ever. When you said in one of the *Black Sparta* stories that the ripe apples 'flumped' I didn't quite like it and it's one of the things I much dislike in my own stuff. Here all's fused, it's easy yet noble.

I haven't read all the stories yet. 'Maiden Castle' is absolutely wonderful—about nothing and all about everything. 'A Matter of no Importance' you've handled more or less before and as movingly; then why is it this time so amazing? The style I say.

You may after these academic tributes think I can't tell you what is the 'common idea' running through the book. But I can. The stories are about loyalty—if we have once given our heart to a person or a hope it matters very much if we withdraw it, the barbarians say. Whereas to the civilised man life is full of justifiable treacheries. At our own level of education I can think of scarcely anyone whom I've known well who has for the last thirty years run straight according to barbarian codes. Of course the barbarians break their own codes but in doing so they break themselves; the civilised man has learnt that there is no consistency even in the heart; he has tripped over his own equipment once again, he is bruised and sad, still he begins to know that this is the human equipment and he picks himself up. Treachery is no longer a ritual act with special consequences. The skeleton of loyalty has been seen through the God-like flesh which is all that barbarians can see and it isn't wholly adorable.

I wish that a barbarian or barbaric hope would love me and ask for my love. But this will never happen. There's civilisation including civilised war. And here are we without either the luxuries or penalties of loyalty, trying to look into our own minds and our friends' without horror.

Having left this letter unposted for a day or two I now feel that it's all off the lines. However, I send it as it will at all events let you know how awfully good I think the stories are.

He ends with a P.S. asking me if I have any influence with Harcourt Brace to try and keep up their interest in Gerald's book.

This thing about loyalty was an extremely potent idea for him. Morgan's books are so much about treachery—this is usually an essential part of the violent happening that comes sooner or later into all of them. But often there has been a counter-treachery, sometimes a deeper but perhaps less visible loyalty, as in 'The Celestial Omnibus' or 'The Other Kingdom'. I wish I could have talked to Morgan at a much later stage about the barbarian loyalties which I found in Botswana and which would have interested him deeply.

In 1938 Morgan writes: 'Joe tells me you are giving a party Thursday. I hope it won't matter if I happen to turn up rather late and not in evening dress.' This was Joe Ackerley. But I cannot even imagine Morgan in really respectable clothes; it would have been quite all right if we had been dressed up in aristocratic Indian gear.

Again, but later in 1938: 'I look forward to the Boat Race, I always do. Could I bring two friends with me?—one weighs a lot, the other doesn't so this will equalise the strain on the roof. Drop me a p.c. if I may: I don't like bothering you but I don't approve of gate-crashing.' We must have met at another party of which he says: 'I enjoyed it myself but couldn't help reflecting that the left wing either knows no working class people or else doesn't regard them as suitable guests.'

The next letter is early in 1939, at a time when Gerald Heard had taken himself off to America and broken with most of his old friends. Morgan says:

> I felt exactly as you feel but forced myself to write to him care of his publishers and the result is a long, affectionate and of course interesting reply. I will send it to you when and if it comes back from France where I have lent it. They are all learning to see with their eyeball muscles instead of their eyes as far as I can make out. The worst of it is the stupider you are the quicker you learn and this is holding back Aldous, though Constance Collier does marvels. I look

> forward to Boat Race day if it comes and suppose it will be all right if I turn up with a child which isn't my own.

This curtain that came down between us and the ones who went to America became worse during the war. In 1940 he writes: 'No, I don't hear from Gerald now or from any of them. I think they ought to write to us but I believe that they find us all so unhappy and so odd that they are scared. I shall write again to them and pull their leg a bit—I fancy they all stand upon one.'

But things were going badly both for Europe and for me personally in 1940.

> I think there are times when it is almost impossible to bear up against a private knock. I have had the good luck not to have one since the war started. I expect, Naomi, you will soon recover, though you feel for the moment you won't and will again believe in what is natural for you to believe in. . . . Perhaps the staircase is going up really, I don't know and can't know. All I can do is to 'behave well' on it with the full knowledge that my behaviour cannot alter the course of events. My rules for my own good conduct are a little strange and may divert you. They were in my mind when your letter arrived—
>
> Obey orders,
> Ignore advice,
> Do not advise,
> Help your neighbour,
> Be interested,
> Don't listen in.
>
> These are not precepts of the future but they do summarise what has been most suitable in my own behaviour during the last ten months.

He ends: 'I look forward to hearing from you again with the news that your health is better and you feel more up to going on. For go on we must, carrying forward our scraps of the past with the future, though we don't know whether the future can use them.'

A KIND OF PROPHET

ABOUT THE MIDDLE of the long weekend when we had recovered from World War I but were not yet ready to face World War II, it seemed as though Gerald Heard was saying something—writing something—which was at the back of all our minds, of extreme importance but so far unexpressed. In fact he was our prophet. I don't think he wanted to be; prophets seldom do. But he was driven into it, perhaps overconvincing himself. We are all liable to do that.

Gerald first came into my ken I think in the mid-Twenties when he was acting as secretary to Sir Horace Plunkett who had for a time been so successful in starting agricultural co-operatives and was much revered in the co-operative movement. By that time H.P., as we always called him, was getting past his prime and often ill but struggling to go on with the work to which he was devoted. Gerald, who was shepherding him about fairly continually, apologises once for leaving a dinner party abruptly when H.P., who had particularly wanted to talk with my Aunt Bay, was suddenly overwhelmed by exhaustion. Another time they were on a sea voyage back from the Cape, and Gerald writes me a long letter about social morals:

> The practical will maintain that all morality is a sham and of course having no instincts, only complex passions, will make an awful mess and a worse reaction. . . . Gradually we can extend credit soundly but at present we must be content with an honest 'this do and thou shalt live'—social hygiene, and for the advanced, small doses of neat altruism as they can stand the drug and really assimilate it. But to start a child straight off on the Sermon on the Mount—Catholic practice—persecution, inhibition, cruelty and ritual, is to give a baby a dose of nectar and neat brandy which naturally he promptly

> emits and is none the worse save for a slight shock, until he learns it's the only refreshment going and begins to nip again. Poor H., he is a constant death's-head warning against the old philanthropy. . . . I remember Bateson saying that if we really relieved life of all its taboos and only exacted the minimum from people all might have not only so much enjoyment that life would be undoubtedly worthwhile, but all would have such full exercise of their capacities and potentialities that the baulking and frustration and sense of having missed the meaning of it all would be absent at life's end and death would not be dreaded. God! What a letter.

Yet through all this he was finding his way gradually towards a different statement, entirely his own.

In another letter he writes about Morgan Forster and Lowes Dickinson: 'Such a perfect hellenist.' Well, in a sense. He goes on:

> But perhaps you don't like the Greek view of life? When you write of 'unreal things like the Parthenon' and 'the real hellenism, friendship and justice and argument' then I capitulate, though out of the best fragments of antiquity we construct a reflector to project it from the past. The news about the new book is the most important thing in your letter—judge then how important it must be. But somehow I do dread the runes and the magics and all that and from a hellenist—why, it's gothic revival, and you'll be in danger of incarceration in Otranto, self-inflicted. In true English doric I am moved to cry 'Coom awt of it' before the crazy ruin falls.

He goes on to tell me about the Elmhirsts about to start Dartington School and looking for pupils who are to learn all the theoretical through the practical. Would I be interested?

He must have been happier about my attitude to Hellas after I sent him a copy of 'Pythian VIII' in typescript soon after I had written it. He writes:

> Dear Naomi, 'Pythian VIII' is as good as any Mitchison which is to say that it seems perfect to me. It's cathartic so one gave up quite early hoping for happiness or even quiet endings. The only thing I'd like added would be a little more of the old. Couldn't you render it cf. S. Benson's dramatic poem to Kwanyin at the beginning of *The Poor Man*—either at the beginning or the end entire for us barbarians? You're necromancing Greece for us and when we're so magical is the time to give us the classic text you've spelled with.

He too admired Stella Benson, to whom far off in China I sent his books.

There is a postscript about lunch and a guest he has asked, Christopher Wood, a musician. 'He has long wished to meet you, being a reader of your works, has nothing to do save play piano, etc. Lacking (through parental foresight in accumulating and then dying) economic urge, wavy hair, twenty-six and somehow appealing—lady be kind.' A few years later, after H.P. died, Gerald moved in with Christopher.

But now he was beginning to do the endless research necessary for his own writing. *The Ascent of Humanity* was published in 1929. I think he was very uncertain about it, bothered that it wasn't exactly what he meant, wondering for a long time whether it was worth sending to a publisher. He goes on worrying in his letters to me; many of these are undated, but several must be from around 1930. In one he writes: 'If I am ever the slightest value as an off-chance speculator it will be more owing to you than to anyone else. . . .' Then he goes on to talk about me:

> I do find I wish very keenly that you mayn't be hurt at Oxford. God, how painful life is! One never seems to stir a finger without getting it so pinched that one can't write for a week. You don't think I'm not really anxious about it all? But my own twists have been so bad that I can only hope for people I'm fond of that they won't get caught.

In the next letter he speaks of Joe Ackerley and Lionel Fielden and then about Christopher:

> My child just back from Berlin. My brother wretched about his finance and his church. Two other friends quarrelling and in tears because they love each other but can't understand each other. In between hearing these confessions I've buried myself in my silly book just to get the sadness out of my mind for a few hours and to speculate on a way out. I'm still sure it's somewhere if one can find it. . . . Do understand that I am twisted by all this pain and only hold on because giving way is worse. It is possible to cheer people sometimes, even when one knows it's at most an impertinence to try.

He ends by saying 'How brilliant that paper of Dick's was. What a mind.'

Once he was in London permanently I expect we usually telephoned. I was often at their flat and found I could usually cure Christopher's headaches by a bit of hand magic. In a letter dated 1931 Gerald writes:

> The real problem in my life seems to be that the people I have been sent to look after can't bear divided attention. It was so with H.P. and now with C. The result is that I feel keenly how much I have had to lose with companionship which I value certainly not less highly. I suppose it's all part of that pruning which is life. If you do something you mustn't do something else. I suppose it's a choice that everyone has to make but keeping that balance between the exclusive and the generous is very difficult. Please don't think that I don't get from your company refreshment as well as amusement and all the best things I associate with the word company. . . . H.P. is very active and I have twice as much work as I can do. I hope there will be a slacking but I'm always (busy or slack) being influenced by you and grateful for it. So much so that I find it hard to imagine I'm any use to you but thank you for that too. Yours, G.

In another letter he talks about love affairs obviously in answer to something I had written and how these complicated relationships mean a great deal of work: 'That seems a real difficulty and why the ordinary people stick to the simplest possible relationship but in any other it is so hard to make things work, not to have to think of one person but two or three, it's theological in its complexity.' He speaks of his homosexual friends:

> Every one of the men I know has tried hard just to have as many affairs as came along and some that needed a good deal of going out of the way to get and a few have really become 'oncers', a state very interesting I should say to an anthropologist but as far as I can judge rather painful to the oncer. In consequence then, with a portentous amount of discussion there is growing up the belief that vows of some sort are necessary. The first tentative effort is the two promise that for two or three months they will keep each other for each other so as to be worth something to each other, otherwise not only has neither been able to show that he can give up anything for the other but they come to each other physically tired and emotionally distracted. Whether after that we shall be able to go further and a threesome be formed, I don't know but it certainly would present a cube increase of resistance. The two can always combine against one in a threesome. So at present the next step back from promiscuity seems one at a time.

And again later in the same letter, which for once is typewritten and so still completely legible: 'Love of two or three or four must be vowed just as much as love of two.' He goes on:

> I don't want to be quite useless to you and if the experience of these comets among whom I live and the conclusions I draw from their orbits are any use to you on your path between them and those that hug the sun of tradition, it will be a weight off my mind, for I see how difficult things are sometimes. It seems lately all the nice and truth-facing people seem so deeply struck and divided that a grim stoicism seems the

only alternative to a scuttle. . . . I've just met a Bengal Lancer and he says most things could be done with deep breathing. I expect we're all rather out of psychic training and that makes living harder.

Meanwhile his books and those of one or two other influential people were helping to build the moral climate of the Thirties. After his *Ascent of Humanity*, published in 1929, the next continued the same impact, in 1931. They were widely read. The general thesis was the historical growth of the individual out of the soulless mass of very early mankind. Yet the soulless mass seemed to have had a generalised non-individual consciousness and the new individuals lost this and instead developed greed, power and war. Yet as the new individuals grow and achieve more understanding and the more advanced moral sense they can begin to attempt to transcend individualism into something automatically other-regarding (that is loving) because each of us is we. In fact we have to go back to a more primitive social feeling and make it come real in modern terms. All this was new in the late Twenties when we had barely stopped regarding liberal progress as inevitable and much to be commended. We were all hooked on technology and had not begun to question it.

In Gerald's search for sources to prove his thesis he read all over the place, as Aldous also did, but with less scientific-family-based scepticism. Auden, in one of those poems of his that used to range over the contemporary scene, spoke of 'noble amateurs like Gerald Heard'. Can we re-read Gerald's books? Doubtful. Some of what he says is now taken for granted and no doubt he helped to make it so. Other aspects are clearly not in accordance with evidence which we now accept. Anthropology in particular has advanced into new concepts. I would question many of his views on history, particularly those on the English seventeenth century. But the books throw out sparks, especially perhaps *The Emergence of Man*, his second.

The Source of Civilization, the third important book, was published in 1935 when it seemed as though only an enormous last-minute effort could save us from utter destruction. But it pointed the way towards a breakthrough into a layer of super-consciousness, for which of course there is plenty of evidence, but because it is dangerous thinking we feel it best to turn our backs and get back into safe old neurophysiology. It is all, I think, still clearer today than it was forty years ago, but is still unacceptable.

It is always dangerous to pick to pieces common sense, including the notion that war should be considered as a normal human activity, though this is historically incorrect. The successful mystic is not able to communicate the essentials or only to a few followers who already see part of the way. I don't know whether in the end Gerald became a complete mystic, whether he crossed the bridge; he seems to have part-persuaded a fair number of people to make the effort to throw accepted reality out of focus in order to perceive the wider field.

In 1931 some of us were thinking along these lines, first of all in terms of possible group-mindedness or group communication—the next step possibly before the much bigger breakthrough to universal consciousness. It was because of this kind of interest that I occasionally went to seances, once or twice with Gerald, but I always felt there was something phoney about them, though perhaps there wasn't. But the messages from beyond were always incredibly trivial. I still don't see the kind of trickery which could have worked some of the seance experiences; I am inclined to think they were genuine but pointless.

However, we thought we ought to try to work out some kind of reaching out to group consciousness and as a start we decided that we would meet and discuss this and we would always and only speak the truth to one another. We called ourselves the Engineers Study Group because several of the members were engineers who had become interested, partly no doubt because they were on the brink of making and using thinking machines—computers. But not all of us, however much we wanted to be absolutely truthful, were good at expressing ourselves. A good engineer isn't necessarily a good talker. It was, all the same, from this group that I got my contact for arms for Spain. I didn't tell Gerald but he didn't ask.

I spoke to a number of people about our project. Some, including

Olaf Stapledon, were deeply interested but could not come regularly to London. Havelock Ellis was also much interested but wrote about *The Emergence of Man*: 'There could hardly be a book which I so much disagree with as his and yet so much sympathise with'.

Morgan Forster wrote:

> I should have been more willing to join the group at other times. For the moment I am contented and happy—I don't think this is the moment, for contentment is not infectious and so I couldn't help. It's this, not my self-consciousness that holds me back. You will all of you be self-conscious and it is one of the things you will probably learn to get round. You will do better the more you get worried by something external as the early Christians were by Rome. A fall in the pound may serve.

Professor Catlin was deeply interested and wrote to both Gerald and me asking sensible questions like 'Are you prepared to meet once a week, once a fortnight, and see if these ideas come?' Lady Rhondda asked for articles on the whole thing for *Time and Tide*. Gerald himself wrote to me about others. Eddie Sackville-West had written that he was 'passionately interested' but Gerald himself was definite that the group mustn't be 'fissured with personalities'. His letter goes on:

> I want to try for one hour a week, twelve, silence, semi-dark. Each, after, sets down comments—but that's simply for later guidance and experiment. Each time a small change might be tried. A collation before one meeting. Complete dark at another. Music at a third. I think the first groups will have to sacrifice something of their own satisfaction to their obligation to be experimental.

Well, that was that and for all the various reasons which one can think of it just didn't work. I head the envelope with the letters in it *The Group That Failed.* Afterwards I retreated back increasingly into politics and putting my faith into some kind of political or economic cure for our evils. That didn't work either.

But Gerald had chosen the way he had to take. The last letter I have speaks for itself; in fact I had made the fatal compromise, in good company no doubt:

> Thank you for your kind letter. I thought when you wrote about tea you said we won't discuss Spain so when D.* brought it up I tried to get him to tell us his views as I thought then you would pass us on to something else; wanting not to discuss it arose not from indifference either to it or to you. On the contrary I feel so much both for the suffering there and for how you must be feeling about it that it was respect not aloofness that advised silence. When the patient is suffering from a deadly disease which his friends believe to be curable by the hedge doctor there are few more painful things than to have to stand by convinced that the diagnosis is incorrect but aware that their devotion and hope is founded on the belief that a simple and quick cure is possible. To tell them crudely that the real state is one which may easily lead to death seems to them only a wish to be unhelpfully superior. I am convinced that the way civilisation is going is fatal and the usual remedies only inflame the disease but I realise as clearly as you do the real cure is the greatest difficulty and needs entire effort. I can only ask you to believe that I am doing all I can to try and do what in me lies towards helping that cure. Anyone who is so trying is acutely aware of the insufficiency and also realises that arguing does little good and much harm. For these two reasons they are anxious not to keep on advising others as to what should be done in particular cases but to try to set about living such a life that new human relationships may finally become possible. There is no short cut and we all make blunders and impatience. Please forgive me. Please also apologise for me to D. I did not mean to be discourteous to him but I felt that to discuss Spain by itself would be no use and to discuss the deeper facts of which Spain and pacifism are only symptoms is impossible

* I am not sure who D. was—it might have been Denny.

unless there is agreement as to certain basic principles and also a will to implement them. That I realise I have no right to expect either of him or you. Again my regrets.

You think, well, better not to see one another for a few weeks. And then it is not a few weeks. It is forever. But it is certainly easier to practise deep meditation and the crossing of psychological barriers for someone who does not have a husband and children and a house and a number of practical commitments. I went my way, he went his. He never wrote from America. Perhaps both of us were hurt.

THE BRIGHT STAR

I HEARD ABOUT the bright new star, young Wystan Auden, from Dick Crossman, who showed me some early poems, and I thought at once, this is it, and made contact. In a while I got him to send me some poems to be published in *The Realist*, just before it perished from lack of financial backing.* The first letter of his which I have must be from 1929 and reads:

Dear Mrs Mitcheson,
I hope you will excuse my writing to you. Do you by any chance know of a job for me? Anything from nursing to burglary: Is it possible to get into a publishing firm in any capacity? If you should know of anything I should be most grateful if you would let me know. Also could you come to lunch next week, any day but Tuesday?

Yours very sincerely
WYSTAN AUDEN

Instead I asked him to tea and suggested that he coached Murdoch, who had been ill following diphtheria, and needed to pick up on Latin. When he came I used to see that he got a solid tea with scones or crumpets or cake. That year he helped to decorate our big Christmas tree, standing nice and tall, able to reach the top branches, on the stepladder; Lois rushed in to say 'Look at my new knickers!' She was the age when one loves frills. I'm not sure how much Latin Murdoch learnt, but they got on.

I have two letters from him from Birmingham in 1930, one written just after Val was born:

Dear Naomi,
I suppose you have just had your baby and so are very

* See below, p. 169.

introverted and don't want letters. Also I am much too miserable at having to leave Berlin to write a decent letter.

I am so glad affairs and you both are turning out well. The poem is bad, I think, but it doesn't matter. You were feeling very lyrical I imagine.

I start term again on Sept. 4th. You must come and see me there. Address

Larchfield
Helensburgh, Dunbartonshire.

It will be great fun seeing you again. I shall probably exhaust and shock you with Berlin confessions. Remember to come.

best love to you, Murdoch and the New one.

WYSTAN

I probably was rather shocked, but would have taken care not to show it. The poem I had sent him, on rereading it after more than forty years, strikes me as rather good.

Now come several letters from Larchfield. He was rather lonely and cut off there. In one he asks if he can come and stay (that year we were at Craignish Castle, which was let for the summer in those days). What an attractive young man he looked! But I had by now given up all hope of match-making. He wanted to move. Dartington was a possibility. He writes:

My dear Naomi,
I've had a letter from Curry. Friendly but doubtful. I've written an answer about Dominicans and Glory which I imagine will pretty well dish my chances. . . .

and then:

I really want to go to Ottershaw College, the place started by the man who was sacked from Bryanston. According to Edward Upward, who is there, it's the buggers dream; a cross between Mädchen in Uniform and The Castle.

Much love and thanks.

WYSTAN

In 1930 I did what I have never done for anyone else (or for myself). I went to great trouble over a first review of his *Poems*, which I wrote at length and with very great care. I arranged for this to come out immediately after the publication of the book, so as to make other critics sit up and take notice, in the *Week-end Review*, which was then very well thought of with Gerald Barry a most competent and sympathetic editor. I also spoke to a few top critics. Wystan wrote:

Dear Naomi,
Thanks awfully for your letter and the very kind review. Any reviewer who tells people to buy the book has said the right thing.

I don't honestly think that psycho-analytic knowledge would help the critics of 'Paid on both sides'—at any rate emotionally. But I do think literary knowledge of the Mummers' play with its Old-New year symbolism is necessary.

I'm very thankful you didn't quote from 'Which of you waking early', which I tried to have removed from the book. I think there are good things in it but as a whole poem it is paupers trash.

I have nearly finished a new play which I believe will be the best I can do just now.

I'm looking forward to seeing Valentine and yourself sometime soon.

Please give my love to Murdoch when you see him.

Love
WYSTAN

P.S. The Listener Book Chronicle says: 'As for Mr Auden we dare not even hazard a guess what his book is all about.'
Am I really so obscure? Obscurity is a bad fault. Re the lines you quote:

<table>
<tr><td>'To breast the final hill'
'θάλασσα on the tongue'</td><td>} deferred ?? asymptotic movement
towards emotional satisfaction</td></tr>
<tr><td>'Snatch at the Dragon's tail
To find the yelp its own'</td><td>} The result of repression
the divided self
Puritan right and wrong</td></tr>
</table>

This is, of course, slightly different from what was actually in the book! And of course he was being extremely obscure, putting in private images all the time. He became better about this later on, but always demanded a bit of hard work and education, especially in the classics, from his readers. Rather an adolescent attitude. He came and stayed and was always a charming guest, nothing wrong with his manners. His next letter says:

My dear Naomi,
I haven't the time to write you a poem just now so it will have to be the ordinary bread and butter letter.

I did so enjoy my stay: but it's no good saying so unless you felt that I did. I hope I put it across to those lower centres.

Here is the photo of the games master on his holiday. What will Lev make of it? I have actually started your article.

The boys are as usual. The head has shingles. I'm expecting to see —— to-night so my heart goes pitter pat pitter pat. . . .

Lots of love to you
WYSTAN

The Orators was published in 1932, but a letter about it is dated August 1931, so he must have sent me the MS to read and comment on:

Dear Naomi,
Thank you for reading *The Orators* so promptly: here are the marginal notes; of no more use I fear than those to the Song of Solomon. . . . In a sense the work is my memorial to Lawrence; i.e. the theme is the failure of the romantic conception of personality; that what it inevitably leads to is part 4.

Formally I am trying to write abstract drama—all the action implied.

The four parts, corresponding if you like to the four seasons and the four ages of man (Boyhood, Sturm and Drang, Middle-age, Oldage), are stages in the development of the influence of the Hero (who never appears at all).

Thus Part 1. Introduction to influence.

Part 2. Personally involved with hero. Crisis.

Part 3. Intellectual reconstruction of Hero's teaching. The cerebral life.

Part 4. The effect of hero's failure on the emotional life.

The litany is the chorus of the play. I am now writing the second half, which is the situation seen from within the Hero. It is in the form of a *Journal of an Airman*. The flying symbolism is I imagine fairly obvious. The chief strands are his Uncle (Heredity-Matrilineal descent and initiations) belief in a universal conspiracy (the secret society mind) kleptomania (the worm in the root). I am finding it very difficult but am getting along slowly. . . .

WYSTAN

Please introduce me to some nice people in Scotland. I don't know a soul.

He writes a postcard from Shetland:

It was so nice to hear from you again. I should love to come but I have spent all my money and must go home to do some work. I will send you something to see when I return. Some of the scenes in the Prawn King and the String Queen were hotter than anything I've read. My dear, how do you get away with it? It is lovely here. I will write from home. Love. WYSTAN
Give my love to Murdoch.

We corresponded a good deal; I wish I knew what I'd written to him to elicit this answer, perhaps from 1931:

My dear Naomi,
Thank you for your charming letter. I liked *The Corn King* very much indeed. I do wish though you would do a contemporary setting sometime. What is this curious psychological sturk of yours against it? I always feel in reading your work that you are only using those silly old Greeks as a symbol. (After all what earthly interest to anyone is history except as

that) It reminds me of the way buggers speak of 'A *person* I was in love with.'

Talking of which I agree with much of what you say but not all. Homosexuality is on one side a naughty habit like thumb-sucking. I can see very clearly your suggested wife, like Jupien with Charlus. I don't believe in marriage with separate latch keys. If a pair are really in love the circuit is closed. It's only the brother-sister relationship that permits of affairs. Such a relation for the woman is deathly. Again, artificially of course, but there, many homosexuals, I for example have only one prejudice against women, a physical one. I am not disgusted but sincerely puzzled at what the attraction is. (Like watching a game of cricket for the first time.)

Yes, please come to Helensburgh, I shall be there after Sept. 8th. I shall look forward very much to seeing you. I don't think any of the Scottish nationalists are any use. McDiarmid is such a fearful intellectual snob and prig.

Here is something; can you read it?

best love
WYSTAN

P.S. Love to Murdoch

I was now getting him to go ahead with the article about writing for my *Outline for Boys and Girls*, to which the next letter refers:

Dear Naomi,
So glad you are better. Term ends here 24th. Could you come up for a week-end before then? Doubtless you've heard about Gerald's trip with me to Dartmoor. Nil desperandum in sano corpore.

The MEMORIAL. How can you be so cold about it. If it is not at once recognised as a masterpiece, I give up hope of any taste in this country. By far the best novel outside Lawrence since the war.

Here is the article. I hope now it's done with for good.

Little news here. The house with the fives court has been

burnt down. The headmaster's wife has taken to climbing trees. I have finished a poem of some length. —— is well, but he has a chilblain, poor darling.

Best love,
WYSTAN

P.S. If you must say anything about me, which I deplore, say this and this only:

Wystan Auden (b. 1907) writes poetry and teaches at a school in Scotland.

I had of course to okay with the authors of the *Outline* what I said about them. My contributors were, I think, rather badly paid. I had hoped they would get a bit more if the book went into another edition, but the clerical opposition stopped that and it was never taken in America. Probably it was too British, encouraging people to think for themselves, instead of telling them just what to think.

The next letter, of 1932, is after his move to Colwall:

Dear Naomi,
Thank you for your letter. The Outline raised the wind.

I agree with the Bishops that Christianity should not have been omitted.

This school is incredible. You'd love it. I teach English, Arithmetic, French, Gym and Biology. 'Sir,' said the head of the school, 'I'm very interested in reproduction.'

Our form is starting a geological museum in aid of the unemployed.

The school is a mixture of The Plumed Serpent and the Church Lads Brigade. Lots of gags and thigh slapping. Also we have a Bach choir. We play the Dragon School. Are any of your offspring in the team?

I am very hard worked but am pegging away at my epic. Why not come and visit me?

Best love,
WYSTAN

Our money comes from chocolate. Mrs Head is a Cadbury.

I went over to see him at Colwall, and we walked over the Malvern Hills. He quoted line after line from *Piers Plowman* and these seemed to go completely into the rhythm of these English hills, the rise and fall. I cannot read it now without remembering them and Wystan's voice speaking the lines.

The next letter is in rather illegible pencil:

> My dear Naomi,
>
> I have never thanked you for the diary, which I read with great interest and was much moved.
>
> . . . . .
>
> How are you? Overworking as usual I suppose. I'm off to the Carpathians this summer, stimulated I believe by childish memories of Dracula. I hope we get interned.
>
> I have a car now and a summer complexion, but am getting too stout. The epic has turned into a dramma which is coasting along slowly.
>
> With much love from your rich, bourgeois and wickedly happy
>
> WYSTAN

I think this was written in 1934 or '35. He refers to my *Vienna Diary*.

After this came his 1936 journey to Iceland. He wrote to me twice from Keswick after that:

> Just got your letter. Yes, of course, send the poetry along. I don't know that I can do much except give my opinion, but I'll do all I can.
>
> I went to see Agamemnon last Sunday and I'm afraid I shall miss you. The translation is lovely, but there is some bloody dancing. I *hate* all ballet.
>
> Am up to the ears in a sort of travel book about Iceland. I've never enjoyed writing anything so much before, but I expect that's a bad sign. I'm looking for a W.E.A. job in Yorkshire next year, so sow the seed for me.
>
> Love
> WYSTAN

The next says:

Dear Naomi,
Thanks so much for your card and your letter which I ought to have answered but was extremely busy producing Cocteau's Orphée in English. It was a great success. The Dance of Death is meant for acting not reading. It depends so much on the music and the dancing to give it body.

My brother is coming to London on Jan. 2nd (next Tuesday) and would like to see you. Could you possibly ask him to lunch and again if possible ask the Russian Ambassador or someone who knows about Geology in Russia to meet him. He and I would be most grateful if you can manage this. Tuesday is the only day as he is sailing on the Wednesday.

I shall be in town sometime early next month and am looking forward to seeing you. Love to all.

WYSTAN

John, Wystan's climbing brother, came to see us and to ask if we could help with a Russian visa as he wanted to climb in the border lands of the northern Himalayas; it was not even certain where the frontier went. I remember a marvellous map he showed us with hundreds of miles between the names of peaks, blank, untrodden, no roads, no passes, the stuff of pure romance—to me at least.

Wystan and I talked about poetry occasionally. I remember him saying that poetry was the most economical way of expressing anything. I would agree, so long as the anything was something complex and mixed with the unconscious, but not if it was a straightforward economic, scientific or, say, agricultural statement. But he wasn't thinking of that. He was extremely good on stress, having, I suppose, absorbed Bridges, even if he disapproved of him later. Equally, he relished assonance, as an Eng. Lit. man should, but sometimes doesn't. At Larchfield he was fascinated by the metrical version of the Psalms which is of course his pattern for 'Not father, further to prolong'. He took things up, delicately, observed them, perhaps used them, discarded them. I don't think he did that to me, at least not consciously, but his world became increasingly elsewhere.

After *For the Time Being* I liked Wystan's poems less and less, which no doubt places me. He and his friends were very critical of my poems; perhaps I should never have shown them to any of them. I don't suppose Wystan would have liked my later books, any more than I liked his later poems. After he went to America we met or corresponded rarely, though I do have one letter written from Swarthmore, Pennsylvania, in 1943, which contains these sentences:

> A letter from England always makes me feel a little queer. Superficially, yes, one does feel cut off, but at a more important level, no. It's rather like a relation with one's parents in later life. It's not easy to be consciously confidential but the understanding is there all right. . . .

Writing about America, he says: 'I never knew, even in Germany, what anti-Semitism meant till I came to this country. All the same I like it here just because it is the Great Void where you have to balance without handholds . . .' But he ends with a P.S.: '*Very* homesick for English Country.'

STELLA FAR OFF

IT MAY WELL be time for a Stella Benson revival, though I wouldn't know myself, because rereading her books brings me up with a bump against a lot of emotions which are unsuitable for my age and experience. I should no longer have them but there they are, alive and squirming, so that I am immediately and uncomfortably half pulled back into the emotional reactions of somebody I no longer am. Perhaps the best thing is to begin by quoting my own first letter to her.* As always I didn't put a year date but it is from River Court so it must have been in the mid- to late Twenties:

> Dear Madam,
>
> I have just finished reading *Pipers and a Dancer* and I must write and say thank you. I don't think anyone has ever quite caught that terrible showman before and you've done it perfectly; it is so infinitely more intelligent than the James Joyce method. But of course—as far as I am concerned at least—you have done it in every book: just got hold of something unsaid about life and crystallised it. This book is even more exquisitely done than the others and that is saying a lot; one sees it all completely except possibly why she got as far as getting engaged at the beginning; I wish you'd defined that more; you could have and it's awfully short as it is. I love all your Chinese descriptions, the people passing, the clothes, the weather; I don't know if you want one to like your descriptions as much as that—I don't think it interferes with one's acute pleasure in the story. I think I have read all your *Star* articles and the thing about war in China that came

* The reason I have it in front of me is that Stella kept all my letters and after her death her husband, James O'Gorman Anderson, sent them back to me with a note to say that she had valued them.

out in the *Athenaeum*; I wonder if you are ever going to reprint them.

My brother wrote to me from India about *This is the End*—it was the first of them that I read; I suppose we made ourselves into Q and J there—it was queer to find someone who knew what one's imagination was like better than oneself. You must have done that for a good many people. Then I read all the others. You do have the right views about magic—it won't quite keep out of anything you write.

This must all be very dull to read. I wonder if we shall ever meet; the Spring Rices, who are our best friends, tell me about you sometimes. And I expect I'm not the only one whose first thought when the news came of war in China was 'what's happening to Stella Benson?'

Yours sincerely,
NAOMI MITCHISON

Her answer headed 'Chinese Customs Mengtz, Yunnan, China' reads:

Dear Madam (I don't feel like beginning Dear Madam in answer to your charming letter but *you* began like that and I have no choice since your signature is a little ambiguous),
I am most grateful to you for writing and it is an enormous pleasure to me to feel that my books are liked by the kind of person I imagine you to be. I do like people to enjoy the descriptions of the things I see. I should not even mind if the descriptions drowned the story since to me my own eyes seem often to drown my own life. That is the only reason why I write; sight is the only magic thing I have.

Ipsie got engaged to Jacob because she was never real or grown up enough to be alone—or to realise that she could never be turned into a real grown-up person even by a real grown-up husband. I do not believe this is far-fetched or impossible.

We have hardly any war at present in this province only a good many brigands but they don't bother foreigners much.

The Mitchison family in the mid-1930s

Bust of Professor Alexander by Jacob Epstein

Below: River Court

River Court: the front entrance

Carradale

I write from Yunnanfu which is a city with an extraordinary number of things to see. Every niche of every street has something to imagine about. But we don't live here unfortunately, we live in a very lonely place called Mengtz and spoil our minds by having to know about the quarrels and complications of a handful of small French officials.

I am coming home next year for a few months—at least I am going to California to decide what I shall do next. If I ever do come all the way home I hope we shall meet under the encouraging wing of the Spring Rices. Only I imagine I am rather a disappointing person to meet.

Yours very sinceely and gratefully,
STELLA BENSON
(Mrs O'Gorman Anderson)

After this she came to Varengeville and most of the correspondence dates from after that when we had really got to know one another. A good deal of course is about her books, for I remained a tremendous fan. I keep wondering what would be thought of her now, almost all her books have an element of fantasy, sometimes straight magic: the English witch and the German witch in *Living Alone* arguing and weeping high over London on the filmily collapsing cloud while their broomsticks fight above them, and always there is death, sadness, the loss of the immaterial world as the normal world breaks in. It's the touch of what one must call whimsy that would I suggest make her work unacceptable now.

Yet *This is the End* was enthusiastically received by the most reputable reviewers, and Stella could go on counting for another fifteen years at least on good reviews and good sales. Her descriptions are still brilliant: America, China, the 'Brown Borough' in East London, Mitten Island. But her values are of her period. Yet if her suffragette were to be reclothed as an IRA girl and the period adjectives replaced I am inclined to think it would do. It is hard on books that because they do so ringingly catch the echoes of their own period they should date so quickly. My good fortune in writing historical novels is that a toga doesn't date nor does a wolfskin.

The next letter from her is I think from 1926 and is again from far off, Kirin Province, Manchuria. She wants to know about my new baby and tells me about her garden and also about the countryside:

> Irises and azaleas in all the green gulleys under the scrub oaks. And if only Communitska's toothache was better we could ride forth and see more irises and more azaleas. Communitska is my little Russian mare. I don't suppose it ever occurred to you that a horse's is the one profession in the world that cannot be pursued by a sufferer from toothache—there is no room for a bit and toothache in the same mouth. Poor Commie, she walks about with her quivering nose wrinkled into a ghastly smile, the Mafoo sits beside her and strokes her hoof comfortingly or scours the town for little patent Japanese toothache cures.

She is wondering what Macmillan will say about her new book:

> Not that it is one of those bold bad juicy books but there are certainly patches of incipient blasphemy on its otherwise smooth surface. Perhaps even Macmillan is getting used to blasphemy by now.
>
> We went to a Japanese tiffin party on Sunday given in a geisha house. A man danced to us—his best dance was called Ten Pine Trees. He balanced dark green and gold fans on different parts of himself and twisted himself about and became extraordinarily like ten pine trees (of course only one at a time). Each pine tree was tied into more incredible knots than the last. Nobody would ever have thought that one man in a green skirt and a black hori with twenty fans could turn into ten pine trees.

She sends a lovely picture of the man dancing at the end of the letter.

In another letter from the same place she describes going to dinner with missionaries:

The other day it was the missionary swarming season or something and we went to dinner with eighteen of them all at once and Sheamus was slapped on the arm by a young lady missionary and called a naughty man—but no young gentleman missionary did anything of the kind to me. At the Russian dinner parties on the contrary nobody calls me naughty—far from it; our hosts with tears streaming down their faces talk about their good Angliski friends helping them to retrieve their honour (they all imagine that they can blow the Bolsheviks out of Russia with hot air)—and we sing loud Russian choruses and compete in emptying glasses of vodka with one gulp and feel frightfully naughty—even though no one calls us so.

A letter of mine must be the same year. It is written in pencil saying:

Dear Stella,
Your letter came the day Sonja Lois was born which was fun. I was feeling desperately pleased with myself. There had been rather a grim three days beforehand during which the doctors were trying all sorts of horrid ways of inducing her to come. And when she did she took twenty-four hours. However it was all very interesting and one forgets about it fantastically soon: I mean one remembers that there has been terrific pain but all quite remotely as if it had been someone else but one is quite prepared to do it again at once. It's amusing to watch nature getting at one like that. Sonja Lois is really rather a little dear, I think probably I like her better than any of them except Geoff who as eldest was naturally the most thrilling. Just as with him I couldn't quite believe in her at first, she's very dark with a black shock of soft hair, grey eyes, broad shoulders and narrow hips. She is just beginning to look and listen and smile a little. I read your article about the pine tree dancer in the *Star* about a week later and felt as if I'd had a private view first! He must have been queer.

It's exciting about your new book. I suppose it will be the

autumn season. I wonder what it's called. Is Macmillan nice about titles? Cape always wants to alter mine.

I am sending you my poems—I've just had the first copies. Do discount all the vers libre ones—I've got through that now! Since then I've written two or three with your vowel rhymes but they are all rather intime and though I am quite shameless about exposing my own guts I have at least to allow a decent interval before doing the same to my friends! Your Forest in the *Nation* was most awfully good: every word carried its exact weight. It's so exciting (after reading a lot of dimmish articles) to come suddenly on that as if it had another dimension or something, it came so sharply out of the paper. I do think it's the right way to make poetry now. . . . Wade Gery is staying with us this week. He's translating Pindar very well I think into free verse and I have been trying to help. The jolly thing about these early Greeks is the unabashed way they produce platitudes. . . . By the way, have you read *Gentlemen Prefer Blondes*? I suppose so. Of course it's intensely fashionable among the highbrows just now: a book with the most disastrously infectious style. . . . I hope this letter is legible. I've got my inside a bit upside down and the doctors make me lie on my belly like a beast of the field so I can't type.

Stella writes back about writing poems:

You couldn't really write in my style fortunately for you because you are not cold-hearted like me. Everything you write must be positive and everything I write is negative. (This is not being too damn humble; negativeness and cold hearts have their place in the world—you could probably divide the world's saviours into two classes, the ones with cold hearts and the ones with very hot hearts.)

I am being cooked in a sort of pie of American missionaries on board this ship. I am in fact the only scratchy nasty little English bone in all this mass of wholesome good white missionary meat.

> I went up to Tokyo for the day today and tried to get Edmund Blunden to come and have a cocktail with me as, though I have never met him, we have written to each other and I like his work (don't you?). He teaches young Japanese to write English poetry I understand (how or why God knows) at the Imperial University. But today he had no classes and was not to be found so I shall still owe him a cocktail at the day of judgment. . . . I had a most dreadful departure from Lung Ching Tsun—train snowed up a whole day and only finally extricated in the wrong direction so that I got back home again to the bewilderment of the dogs whose fur was not yet dry from the tears I had shed into it at parting. We had to hire two carts and took nearly twelve hours to flounder through twenty-four miles of drifts—some of them so deep that if the drivers did not see them in time the front horses would completely submerge, the carts turn over and poor Mr and Mrs Anderson be coarsely shot into the snow. The result of all this was that I missed my ship to Kobe and had to travel like hell by trains and ferries all down Korea and along Japan in order to catch this ship—which I now wish I had missed too.

In the next letter she has caught up with mine and congratulates me on my baby saying, 'Everybody seems to have babies but me. However, I daresay I should have a gloomy and C3 baby so it is best for its own sake in Abraham's bosom—or wherever it is that non-existent babies live.'

She writes about my book of poems which somehow or other had arrived, saying,

> I thought your poems would be too fiercely sure for me—not cocksure but—well, anyway unwoolly. I feel most at home with woolly thoughts. However, when the book came I loved it and I always shall—it isn't comfortably woolly of course but it isn't that slightly scratchy kind of silk I feared. I like the latter half—and best of all the last poem of all . . . one about me makes me wish most sadly that I wasn't my me but your me. . . .

This of course shows very clearly how little I really knew about Stella's real grown-up life, her anxieties and problems and the kind of choices which she was having constantly to make.

Another letter from her:

> Thank you so much for sending me Simonetta Perkins and Mr Eliot. I am particularly glad to have them both and had indeed been wanting them. There seems to have been a sort of conspiracy to quote T. S. Eliot in various papers just lately and I have learnt to cross myself reverently at each reference without even hearing one entire line of his. Now thanks to you I know all that he allows to be known. These young people make me feel hopelessly left behind. I think a marshmallow must feel like that in the presence of a green olive or a pickled walnut. The marshmallowism of my generation seems all to come out in our verse—we can get quite a pickled tang into our novels but the poems of a person like me seem seriously infected with sweetness and light after reading T. S. Eliot. . . . Don't you think this is rather sweet—a Japanese official here trying to be extremely English in parting from an Englishman: 'Well, goodbye, old chap, and if I don't see you again, hullo'. I think this ought to be adopted by the true Christian as his formula on parting.

I think the next letters must be round about 1929, though again it is rather difficult to date them properly, but in one I discuss rhyme and metre with her, asking about the metre of her poem 'This is the Feast' and going on to talk about G. M. Hopkins's sprung rhythms: 'I don't think he had probably come across syncopation much, otherwise he would have said syncopated. The rhythms are like ordinary ones but the stresses come on unexpected parts of the feet.'

I think Stella's next letter may have been just after that when she says:

> I am a little lost and widowed at this moment James having gone away for three days—left me alone in the middle of this

war while he drives a malarial Swedish friend through the next war into the next war but one to meet a launch and be conveyed to hospital. . . . I am left under the wing of our one remaining white neighbour and if the war gets any worse I shall gently elope with same in his company's launch which is tied to the bund opposite our front gate for the purpose. Meanwhile we sit moodily sipping sherries and playing chess, listening to rumours of war.

I don't think I do write syncopated verses—at least I always write them to tunes and the tunes aren't syncopated (I was looking some of my verses over after getting your letter and singing some of the tunes inside myself)—on the contrary the tunes are rather eighteen-ninetyish and a bit sweet like a canary's song. I cannot repeat too often—I am absolutely not a poet at all—not even poetic, I never could write verses except by mistake and a mistake always arises from a blank technique rather than an overexuberant one. Your little finger knows ten times more about poetry than my whole skull. This isn't humility. I think I am rather a good writer apart from poetry. I am very cocky and smug about my next book. It could easily be better I suppose but not if it was written by me. It is a considerable step towards my ideal impersonality—losing one's soul in order to save it in other words. Yours ever, dear Naomi.

Clearly my next letter is an answer to this. I start by saying,

it was extremely nice hearing from you though I do wish you weren't in the middle of such eventfulness. People all over London have been clamouring to know what has become of you and nobody seemed to have heard for months: you just disappeared like a fairy. It's very good news about the new book; it will be immensely interesting to see how far you can take this method of yours, of standing away and watching your creature sink or swim. . . . I read a paper at Oxford with some of your verse in it (among a lot of others, including much of my own, all in scraps and anonymous) and one single one of the young ones who is really a poet was fearfully interested in yours especially 'Every tree . . .'. He is a man called Auden, aged twenty-two and with any luck the real thing. He uses new and exciting forms and is sometimes difficult to follow. But he has an Elizabethan sense of verbal beauty and I am really rather ridiculously excited about him. He is not beautiful himself because he has the sort of light-coloured eyebrows that don't show at all but he is very charming. And he teaches in a dim school in Scotland. If his poems are published—and I am trying to persuade Faber what a good man he is—I will send them to you.

There are one or two short letters from Stella and a long one from me clearly written from Craignish and beginning 'How ripping of you to send me your book!' I must have been in some kind of a daze when I used that particular adjective. I had apparently brought her book *Living Alone* up to Scotland to read aloud to the children. 'But after I had only just begun reading it aloud Denny took the book away and finished it all in one gulp. Murdoch on the other hand suspected it of not being true.'

I go on:

We are up here in this incredibly beautiful place thirty miles from a station (though obviously that means nothing to you!), all very Celtic, islands and sunsets and sea lochs of blue paint. The gentry are rather alarming—these narrow cruel Highland faces, mouths and eyes a little twisted and arrogant and something too delicate and inbred about their hands and skin. But the farmers are capital red heads and very jolly to talk to, rather less dour than my own coast. We are having a dance next week—it started as a very small show (it was very daring for a mere tenant to do this kind of thing at all) for the estate but apparently it is turning into the event of the neighbourhood and all the farms and housemaids of all the large houses are cadging invitations. The gardener who is running it has produced one of the best pipers on the west coast, also a fiddle and melodeon and

> we shall have to dance all the proper things—quadrilles, reels, Flowers of Edinburgh, Strip the Willow, Petronella and so on.

This was the dance that comes into my book *We Have Been Warned.*

I write about the book on feminism which I was trying to get on to at the time and for which I was collecting materials but I say,

> Goodness knows if I shall ever get it written because I want it to be history and philosophy and political discussion and that may be more than I can do. But I don't want to write another novel for a long time, if ever again. I get more and more interested in events and I am quite sure that the feminist position wants to be restated every few years. There are a whole lot of new problems since the last statement which must be dealt with. . . .

Were there other letters? Surely, but they have slipped away, are no more, have disappeared into the house of living alone. Stella died in 1933; I never saw her again. Her books are in the chilling basement of the London Library, along with a few other good novelists and countless more bad or indifferent ones, much read in their time, now forgotten. Why do we go on writing? Stella would have had a wry answer.

STAR MAKER

BETWEEN OUR QUARRELS my brother and I corresponded quite a lot and even sometimes managed to meet without snapping at one another. If there was anything which really interested us both things went all right. I used to send him my books and clearly he read them with involvement but had to be critical, though he sometimes got cross if other people criticised them in what he supposed was an unfair manner even if I myself hadn't complained!

It must have been in a time of calm that he told me about Olaf Stapledon who had the kind of imagination he really admired. I went straight out, bought *First and Last Men* and got in touch with the author. We swapped books and Olaf began writing in his small, exact, completely legible handwriting, the lines always going straight across the page. In the first he thanks me for sending *Black Sparta*, saying which bits he liked best:

> From experience I know that people generally fail to appreciate what one supposes to be one's best and it may be that you have put more into your verse than your prose. But I can get more out of your prose than your verse so far. The music of your verse delights me and I particularly like the assonances of the child Jason but the stories are better still for me at least.

He had been reading Gerald Heard's book *The Ascent of Humanity* and comments: 'It is brilliant and helpful though there is much in it that seems to me unjustified. I feel very doubtful about his theory of co-consciousness and about spiritualism. All the same the book is very stimulating.'

I must have sent him a copy of a letter I wrote to my godfather, Professor Alexander, about *First and Last Men* in which I said: 'And occasionally he breaks down.' Would I mention some of these places? Clearly I did for his next letter goes: 'I think I really agree with them or most of them now that the book is well away from me and I can see it without prejudice. I hope I shall not make these particular mistakes again. Of course I did best at parts I was most interested in.' He goes on in the same letter: 'Your brother kindly asked me to come and see some of his "vital art" some time. I hope I may also have the good fortune to meet you some time. "Vital" is an overworked adjective but I am sure it ought to be applied to your art as to your brother's experiments.'

We did meet soon after that. He didn't look at all like my idea of a science-fiction writer. He was strong and stocky with light brown northern-looking hair cut short and very blue eyes. There was nothing extraordinary about his clothes. He often looked worried, perhaps because he was looking too far into the future or perhaps because he was on to a problem of which the probable scientific solution was not visible. He was also very conscious of social problems but often uncertain whether the political solutions which were suggested would have the effect they were supposed to. He read a lot of solid science and talked to scientists and listened to them sensibly and intelligently whenever possible.

In the next letter he is fixing up a lunch date with me and Gerald Heard. These lunches became a regular thing, something to look forward to. I often find them when I look back on my old diaries. They were mostly at the Café Royal and I used to get quite cross with Gerald for always choosing the least nice pudding. I still kept a childish taste for the most elaborate ice cream one could get on the cheap menu and Olaf didn't disdain food on his excursions to London. It was always fun too, spotting literary or artistic characters in the Café Royal where so many of them forgathered.

He wrote again in 1932 after I had sent him *The Powers of Light*. Clearly he liked it very much indeed and also, I was glad to see, Eric Kennington's pictures. He writes: 'They surprise one with a kind of tingling satisfaction, altogether the little volume is so alive that I imagine myself getting a sort of tactual pleasure in merely handling it. That is what books ought to be like.'

We saw quite a bit of the whole Stapledon family, including the children. Olaf had just published *Waking World* and must have had an argument with John Pilley and also with my son Denny who by then was in a state of conviction about dialectical materialism. Olaf writes:

> Tell Denny please that the answer to his question 'how do you know that you really believe what you say about religion?' is something like this: I may have madly misdescribed what I feel but *what* I described is at least as immediate as the warmth which I attribute to a fire. I don't believe I am warm; I just *am* warm. Similarly with the 'worship' experience. But *interpretation* of the experience is sure to be mostly false. That is the only answer I can give. But I am not claiming mystical insight.

He has a postscript: 'I am afraid *Waking World* has damned me in the eyes of the scientists. It's sad because I have usually a doglike respect for them. And yet—they are so *sure* of themselves.'

By that time he was at least calling me dear Naomi; he had always been very formal up to then. And in fact our relations always had a sort of gentle north-country formality. Yet I seem to have written to him as a very close friend towards the end of 1935. I suspect I was in one of my usual states of emotional entanglement combined with political doubts which were as devastating as the religious doubts of the late nineteenth century. He writes to me as somebody who cares very much but keeps his head and doesn't rush in with over-sympathy:

> Don't you go the pace too much in everything you do? It's so tempting sometimes because it gives one the sense of being effective. But it's dangerous for people whose real function is to use their minds because it blots out all the more delicate reactions and makes for bad work. At least that's my experience. . . . Apart from overstrain surely there's another thing the matter, don't you think? I may be all wrong, but I suspect that you have come up against a most serious flaw in the

modern spirit. You have taken it all terribly seriously and lived it conscientiously and it alone is not good enough to live by for a sensitive person. It has to be supplemented by something else perennial, not a new discovery. The sense of lack in it drove you to magic, Gerald to yoga, others to Fascism, others to emotional communism—and you too, because all this longing not to be separate is a weakness. You *must* be yourself as precisely as possible otherwise you're no good for community. You are different, 'special', and you must not funk the fact and try to bury yourself in the herd. And the more special people are the more capable they are of real community, not mere herd-mindedness. Community means being intensely oneself and intensely aware of other bright individual selves and acting accordingly. It doesn't mean all howling in unison in a trance. That's what it is for Fascism and the worst sort of Communism. Is this all beside the mark? I think you have to be yourself and damn the consequences. And don't do things that are not your job. And as for books, it's ridiculous to say they're no good. The right ones are just about all that really matters these days. (But then one goes and writes a wrong one! but my next will be a right one and much bigger than me which is odd. But you see it's *making* me bigger.)

Well, as I was saying, there really is something hopelessly wrong at the bottom of this modern spirit, admirable as it is in some ways. It's so hard to sort out the good from the bad in it. But I should say the positive bad in it is this cult of the abstract group, an obsession with herd emotion and sheer funk of individuality. And the negative bad (which is the cause of the other) is what would have been called godlessness formerly but the word is no good today. It's what Spinoza had amongst others and it kept him straight and at peace always. It's a sense of the obverse of human desires, even the best of them. Now I'm talking rubbish and it's post time and I believe I have cracked a rib falling on a rock but perhaps not. . . . Someone said we have to accept ourselves and not try to be somebody different. That's part of it.

Now as then, most of us feel the strain of individual moral or political decisions and tend to shelter in the group. And then we realise that it's so often the lowest common denominator and we run away from it too. This seems to be a perennial human swing and a very painful one for those of us who can see what we are doing.

Olaf wrote to me in the summer of 1940 after my baby died, as most of my best friends did, but he goes on to the state of the world and to talk about Acland's movement for which he was working as much as he could:

> How I hate political work however. And if you hate a job you can't do it well. Nowadays I feel horribly useless and am reduced to doing local ARP and cultivating my acre. . . . I am writing occasional articles (e.g. in *Scrutiny*) and a book but it's all futile now. We must concentrate on keeping Hitler out surely, bad as our present regime is. I think the country is learning its lesson fairly rapidly and there *may* really be a chance of something better after the war if we are not wiped out. . . . My (qualified) pacifism has been put in cold storage. But how loathsome it all is! And of course I remain fundamentally just as much pacifist as before. But at present pacifism won't work. . . .

We wrote to one another fairly often during the war, holding one another's hand so to speak, helping one another I am sure. I have one other letter from him, from 1944, soon after *Sirius* was published. He was worried about the book, no doubt partly worried in case he had been wrong in writing it as he did and yet equally sure he had been right to do so. 'Yes, I know,' he writes, 'I alternate between cold intellectualism and more emotional patches. I always do. I just don't know how to integrate them and both moods are necessary in the sort of stuff I write.'

We probably wrote to one another again, in fact I can remember writing to him about his last book, but I have no more of his letters. When in 1950 he died suddenly in seconds it was like a part of oneself dying.

THE MYTH AND THE MAN

MOST PEOPLE ARE in two minds about having myths made up about them. Wyndham Lewis probably enjoyed it on the whole, especially when it was the myth of the Enemy. But all the same, I am quite sure he enjoyed getting out of it sometimes and just being an ordinary person deeply interested in the technique of his art. I have an idea that this was part, at least, of why he and I got on so well; I think I was good at asking questions about and discussing the techniques both of painting and writing. Of course, he contributed to the myth and gave it some more to feed on if it showed signs of slackening. Did it not in the later years turn its consuming fires on to its own centre?

In a rather different civilisation, one in which the values of youth, including of course the rebellious values, are less important, might he not have been allowed a golden ageing into mature wisdom? He could have been a guru—and not the first guru to lash out occasionally at his stupider disciples. Yet a guru must above all have charity. Only from the basis of charity, that is, of universal love, can the scarring but necessary anger leap. Most people will say he did not have this; I am less certain. Perhaps even if he had lived longer—who knows?

The virtue of charity would seem incompatible with the searing anger of most of his books, especially the later ones. There was this myth of Lewis as the Enemy—everyone's Enemy, not merely the Enemy of the establishment. That version still goes on, but I think myself it is wrong. When the last exhibition of his pictures was happening in London, art critics spoke of his violence and fierceness; the harshness of line that leapt out at one; he could not paint anything lovely. So when the pictures came to Glasgow I took up the drawings he had made of my children, including one of my youngest daughter, then aged five or six. It is a tinted drawing of a pretty child, a child with the underlying bone structure which would make for adult beauty, and was painted with the affection and kindness that some people say Wyndham Lewis never had. No popular 'child portraitist' could ever have done anything so grave and lovely, but it was all finished in a couple of half-hours at the studio. He cast it away and I picked it up from the floor. He was not entirely pleased with it but I, as the child's mother, was, and am.

His drawings of my sons in their teens and of one of them as a child have the same quality. They are drawn with the utmost economy of line and those of the two older boys are still recognisable after forty years as the same people; the underlying structure is there. But the youngest is a brilliant drawing of a child—who is now grown up. I asked him: 'Do you remember being drawn by Wyndham Lewis?' The answer: 'No, but I remember drawing him.' And then I remembered how paper and crayons and encouragement were brought out to help on the sitting.

It is difficult to know about oneself. He did one big portrait of me in oils, in 1938, where I sit stylised and frowning with a notebook. I was writing *The Blood of the Martyrs*. I am frowning because I wanted to go on writing the book and had in fact said that I wouldn't sit for him unless I could go on with it; but he couldn't bear me to move, even move one hand, except in the break—ten minutes in the hour.* He put a crucifix behind me in the picture, somewhat as a tease, while in front, as in several of his studio pictures, is the curved ashtray which was always on the table. I didn't really want that crucifix but now I think he was perhaps right; he knew a bit more about me than I knew myself.

Wyndham's teasing could be very gentle. When my youngest son was sitting to him there were pudding basins here and there on the studio floor upside down. 'There is a mouse', said Wyndham, 'under each of these pudding basins.' So the small boy in

* Forty years later I sat for my portrait to the Australian Clifford Pugh, who congratulated me on my professional approach and ability to take the exact pose after a rest. I said, 'I had to be able to do that, sitting for Wyndham Lewis.'

the picture is frowning with puzzlement; it is probably bluff from this grown-up and if so the sooner he picks up a pudding basin the better. But of course it might be true. This strange man with the pipe and the black hat might really have caught mice and somehow got them under the pudding basins. Meanwhile he has been offered crayons and paper and is drawing the man. Wyndham was so definite about the mice that I was quite shaken myself—yes, there might easily be mice or indeed anything else under those basins. So the child who is going to become a scientist with an enormous programme of research has already the brooding, scowling, intent look.

Another picture of Wyndham's which I have is the resting Ethiopian, a beautiful ebony woman lying on a cushion with one hand out above the blue stream in front of her across a corner of the picture. 'What is she doing?' I asked. 'Picking a dream out of the river.' 'Oh, do put it in!' So he paints in the shape of a dream and the background of the picture has a Greek temple front cutting into a strong pattern of white: this too for me.

Again and again in his writing he would use the language of his myth. 'I enclose a cutting which will detonate you.' I am intended to be part of his myth. And indeed I took his side. I had reviewed *The Apes of God* for *Time and Tide*. That was when our friendship began. I had not known him before 1930 but he wrote to me after this review, which apparently seemed to him more perceptive than any other, partly perhaps because I genuinely knew nothing about the Bloomsbury quarrel, so reviewed the book solely on its merits as literature. I don't think I ever reviewed any of his later books; one reason was because I cared for him more as a painter than as a writer.

He wrote to me quite a bit about his books. This, in July 1931:

> As you see I am here still upon the edge of the Spanish Sahara, baked by breaths from the Sudan, chilled by winds from the Atlantic luckily, too, and gathering much material for an essay upon Barbary—as I expect you know, Beb'rig is probably just Barbary, and I am amazed that Lawrence (D.H.—not the

Colonel) did not find it out. I have been to palaces, and broken bread with people, calculated to lay him out in a foaming ecstasy. At all events, these folk are the Barbarians right enough, and they build the most magnificent castles upon the tops of cyclopean rocks, in the heart of vast mountains. They have to be seen to be believed. And they all poison each other with arsenic whenever they get a chance—even placing arsenic in the babouches (slippers) of their guests, and anywhere else they think it may get into their bodies. Meantime, they are as brave as lions (so the French say) and surely one of the handsomest people in the world. I say 'handsome' and it is of course masculine beauty, but there is a great deal of grace too, always among the men. The women are out of it. I am sure you would enjoy being here very much. Next time I come here I shall go on to the Congo.

But I don't think he ever did.

He also mentions the drawing of me which came out in *Time and Tide*, which was always very friendly towards both of us. I think he sold several of me, one to Leeds, one to 'a musical butcher from Glasgow'. Who? In another letter he says, 'I have been engaged in a close corps-a-corps business struggle for some weeks, but I am emerging victorious.'

I spent a lot of time and energy trying to persuade him that his quarrels were imaginary, that people didn't really hate him or try to suppress him. We used to argue about all this while he did a whole series of drawings of me. This was in the full Enemy period, the spring and late autumn of 1931. In most of these drawings I am wearing a very formal rose brocade dress which I had bought secondhand in Sarajevo. It had a very low neckline and loose silk-lined sleeves cut away in an odd scallop at the shoulder. He was never tired of the shape of that rather stiff dress, held together at the waist with a big golden brooch; but sometimes in the drawings my hair is close to my head in coils over the ears, and sometimes it is in long corn-coloured plaits. I chose for myself one of the most stylised versions, in which he used me in my dress to suggest something else; he called it *The Tragic Muse* and it is one of the finest of his drawings.

Those drawings were all done in the Percy Street studio, where, in the period of the myth, he talked and talked, trying I think to find out if I was or wasn't part of the establishment. In fact I wasn't, but then I was no Enemy either. I was perhaps more innocent than he could suppose. He told stories which showed him in a shocking light. There was one story of a man who chucks a child under the chin and breaks his neck then goes to the father and says 'I only did that', chucking another child under the chin and breaking its neck too. I found that a horrid story—at this time my own life was much bound up with young children—and I couldn't think why he told it me; I also didn't think it was really possible so I didn't worry about it as much as I would have otherwise.

I am still not sure why he told it but perhaps he thought, and thought correctly, that I was too unguarded and believed too much in the innocence of others and, naturally in a left-wing agnostic, in human perfectibility. Perhaps he wanted me to grow up, to develop a certain necessary hard coat of cynicism—necessary even if you retain your original humanism, as I hope I have, because otherwise those with no hard coat get too much hurt. I think this is implicit in a letter dated 11 February 1934, just after he had moved to Scarsdale Studios and obviously about something we had been arguing round:

> You got me a bit wrong the other day—I will straighten that out when we meet. But the seeds of suspicion *must* be sown in the young, I mean the *sheltered* young—because of course the wind is not tempered etc. (all these misleading sententious scriptural proverbs ought to be kept out of their way too); Rochefoucauld is wiser than Solomon. Lane's Arabian Nights, Swift and Samuel Butler ought to be put into their little hands as early as possible. But you know all this better than I do!

He was busily spinning the Enemy myth all this time and of course making mysteries. That was all part of it. He changes his address 'but please remember to mention this to nobody!' Or again,

> I have been delaying writing to you because I could not make up my mind whether I ought to come to your party on Guy Fawkes Night because I might frighten Gollancz—you remember last time he said he was so frightened he wouldn't come into the other room as I was there! But I want to see you and so all I can say about it is that he'll have to have the wind up for once. I shall dress in a tuxedo.

I always felt one had to play up to all this but I never could take it 100 per cent seriously. If I had done that, I would have been bound to be angry with him. So long as I thought of him as 'the Enemy', someone rather like the frightening dancers in West Africa whom the children run away from although they know quite well that they're only their big brothers dressed up and masked, that was all right. But if I took him seriously he had to be my own real Enemy, because he used from time to time to make shockingly fascist or neo-fascist remarks which I as a convinced and earnest member of the Labour Party could not possibly take.

In 1933 we had begun talking about doing a book together. *Beyond this Limit* (my title) was a total delight to do. I think it was my idea to start with, but it developed jointly. I did the writing and he did the pictures but he came more and more into the story as we went on. There were two main characters: Phoebe, who is me, is usually drawn in a wide-skirted, unfashionable, not to say highbrow dress, which I used to wear at the time with a handkerchief knotted over my head—another highbrow fashion. The ticket collector, who is also Hermes the guide of souls, becomes increasingly clearly a self-portrait, especially in the picture where he is clothed 'in authority' as a bishop. The black hat comes in.

The odd thing is that the ticket collector, speaking cynically and behaving roughly to Phoebe, gradually throughout the book begins to show a divine kindness so that the story, even when the characters are all descending out of the Hotel Terminus in the lift that takes them down to the Kingdom of Hades, has a kind of happy ending. Phoebe has seized on the ticket collector about to leave her in the terrible hotel looking out on to ultimate chaos,

> her fingers closing over the badge of his union. 'We've worked together', she said. 'You can't just leave me like this! I won't let you go.' The ticket collector raised his own hands and laid them over hers but did not tear hers away nor rise on wings out of her grasp. 'Of course if you put it like that,' he answered, 'I'll do what I can. . . .'

More than once I had caught hold of Wyndham at his most cynical and annoying and shaken him. And it had always worked out.

We worked on that through the autumn of 1934. It was the greatest fun and I don't think I have ever written better, because he jumped on me like a tiger if I got a word wrong in a sentence, or if I allowed myself to smudge something by over-hasty writing. I saw the drawings as he did them and then that suggested to me where the story was to go to next. We talked it over like children. He writes on 28 December 1934, with a note 'Today is the Feast of the Innocents—*Childermass!*' Then:

> I am back—a few days disagreeable blank and I am working hard again. Today I took a few of the drawings to Howard* to get the work started. On Monday I shall take another batch and by the middle of the month the remainder. He says the blocks of the whole 30 will take *one week* to make. So that will be well *inside the limit.*—the limit in this case being your transatlantic *ticket!*—I am certain you will like the stuff when you see it altogether. Tonight I am doing you a little duck of a drawing of the two winged maidens in flight. It will be a capital set.

I was off to America just then with Zita Baker, and he asks for

* Wren Howard, the partner at Cape with whom we dealt: a delightful person with a sure eye for production.

a copy of the contract so as to have something 'to testify to my rights vis-à-vis Cape'. But Cape treated him right just as they treated me. He went as far as to say he was pleased with them.

Other publishers were less amiable, however, and some literary editors disliked him so much they refused even to print reviews of his books. It seems extraordinary now to think that he could have a show and that I was the only person to buy one of his pictures. (I longed to buy another, which is now in the Tate, but I just didn't have the money.) And it was that way right through the Thirties.

Certainly he did have real grievances, and he found it difficult to realise that many of the younger writers and painters admired him greatly and wholeheartedly. If he had admitted this it might have spoiled the myth of the Enemy in which everyone had to be against him. I remember only once when he was genuinely suspicious of me. I saw it at once when he opened the door with that black hat of his pulled down over his forehead; he was about to let go and slam the door in my face. The only thing to do was to get through by main force and a hard shoulder before he had quite decided; I did just that and threw myself on to his large chest and then somehow it all melted away.

Yet although he trusted me it was many years before I knew he was married and still more before I met his wife and immediately liked her. The many portraits and drawings of her are as kind and gentle as the one of my little daughter. But it could have been difficult for her sometimes, living with an Enemy. Perhaps his wife is the one person who would know if he was tired of the myth before the end. I thought he was. Or did he, when accepting that terrible blindness which came on him so suddenly, accept also a pattern of gentleness and an alarming humility?

I have two postwar letters from the Forties, by which time he was in the Kensington Gardens Studios with a telephone number at last 'but it is very hush-hush—pass on number to nobody'. (He would never have his name in the telephone book and I used to find myself wanting to ring him up from a phone box and not having the magic private number with me.) The first letter is partly about an exhibition, but also about my latest book, *To the Chapel Perilous*: 'The ghostly congregation from the churchyard was beautiful—did you invent it? No matter, your Lancelot is my Lancelot.'

In the next:

> The Highlands—still more the Islands—have a damp and bleak sound to me. But Notting Hill Gate it is true is not much better. I don't understand your reference to my *quarrelling*. Certainly I have been obliged to defend myself on a number of occasions during the past thirty or forty years; but I have never gone out of my way to quarrel with people; nor do I enjoy brawling. If McDiarmid is so quarrelsome as you say it may be just to keep warm up in Scotland or if not possibly a part of his publicity?
>
> There are at least half a dozen people trying to quarrel with me at present. I may be obliged to take some notice of one of them before long; he will then go chattering around everywhere denouncing me as an aggressor. He will be all injured innocence. They tell me McDiarmid's dialect verse is splendid stuff. If that is so, it would cause a lot of people to quarrel with him; and you may get the impression that it is he who is doing it all.
>
> It has made me quite tired thinking of all the 'quarrelling' that I am supposed to have done and that McDiarmid does so I will put down my pen and go and have two teaspoonsful of Metatone. I suppose you would say I am engaged in a quarrel with these bacilli, which have forced their way into my bloodstream? A final word: you have a very good young Scottish artist named Colquhoun.

During the next ten years I saw him quite often when I was in London. Then came the blow—quickly, so that his sight went with a sketch unfinished. He had just written the dreadful description of hell in the last volume of the *Childermass* trilogy, far nastier than Dante's Inferno and that is saying a lot, if one takes the Inferno not as poetry but as a description of eternal torture. Yet when I said it gave me nightmares to read it, he seemed gently surprised—and even pleased.

The last time I sat with him he could hardly speak. I held his hand, hoping it might help. So one is left with the Enemy. For of course one can't get rid of a myth which one has made for oneself any more than Prometheus could get rid of his eagle. So whatever he may have thought of it in the end he will have to live with it in the books of literary criticism and biography and scowl at us from under the wide-brimmed black painter's hat and poke us to see whether or not we are alive.

WISE STEVIE

I GOT TO know Stevie Smith in the Thirties. Probably I wrote to her about her early poems which I liked very much. She looked like a bird, not an exotic bird but one of the plain-coloured English birds, restless hedge skirmishers, good survivors in any weather. But what she said was anything but bird-like; it was witty, full of meaning, one-off from a packed mind.

The earliest letter I think is dated just 'Monday'; it must have been written just after I came back from a curious trip round the Greek islands with Denny, Murdoch and Margaret Cole as my own cabin companion. For she says,

> I hope you have had a lovely time, are quite better again, did not lose too many old ladies, did not drown anyone in the volcano, and didn't wear yourself out lecturing. . . . I am glad you liked some of the poems. Yes, it is a very mixed bag and there are still hundreds unpublished in various hands in various quarters. *A Good Time* represents the scourings of about ten years of elicit office scribbling generally as you will see in a rather unsatisfactory and futile round, or is it square, peggishness. I should like to see you and hear more of what you think of them if it wouldn't bore you. No, no, no, I don't feel like Cleopatra at the moment, I feel just unhuman, tired and rather cross with Hamish. I'll tell you when I see you. (This letter is getting rather libellous.) I had the most awful fight with Cape over the nauseating sum of £2.14.1.—I repeat and a penny, won my point (I'd already fought and won it last September but that is Ganz Gleich the pets Nicht?). Phoebus is getting hot cattish, I mean cat on hot brickish about 'all this yellow paper' and I am beginning to wonder if he will stand for the new novel which Cape liked and will presumably (contract temporarily held up)

publish in the autumn. You are lucky not to have a Phoebus to square. I am getting very devious. Major —— has chosen this inauspicious moment to descend upon his motherland so if there is a slap up libel action over the poems you will keep under cover, won't you. I rely on you implicitly!

How is your woolly dog? Let me know won't you when you have a moment to come and have a talk.

Well, well, I hope the libel action not having happened then won't happen now! The gallant major was one of her problems but she enjoyed the occasional problem salt in her broth.

The next letter is properly dated, 20 May 1937, and she is about to go with Auntie Lion to Hunstanton for an 'early holiday and a rather boring good-for-you one'. Clearly I had written a review, probably for *Time and Tide*, for the letter goes on:

I have wasted sixpence a week on that blasted publication but no sight or smell of your review. I expect it's too energetic for them. I expect they no likee my musee. Shall I ring them up or would that put them still further off? Major —— has pottered over to Dublin and I see his wife and she hasn't guessed so I trot her round and hope for the best.

(You see with what fatal ease I drop into doggerel?)

I must now hand on heart and sackcloth on my back take back formally and publicly all the hard hard things I said about Cape because after a very little, very gentle persuasion from me they have given me a 15 per cent run on the first 5,000 copies of the new novel which isn't so bad plus as advance what the book earns before publication, plus a tearful reminder that thanks to advertising they are still out of pocket over yellow paper. After all this I could only just bring myself to accept the 15 per cent.

It looks as if I must have suggested a change of publishers, for the next paragraph reads: 'No, no . . . I am feeling so very fond of Cape it would break my heart to leave them, Rupert, Hamish and even Jonathan I see now behallowed, *couleur de rose* just this side of sainthood.'

After that I must have written her a gloomy letter. 1937 was a year when various things were going not too well and I was becoming more and more aware of the possibilities of fascism or war. There was already a steady trickle of people, Jewish or socialist, coming into Britain. Stevie wrote back: 'You take me at a disadvantage. If only I had my typewriter with me!' Like me she always preferred to type letters, felt somewhat maimed if she had to write by hand.

She goes on:

> No, I don't think we can pass the buck to forces of evil or to anything but our own humanity. We are bloody fools. But then we are hardly out of the eggshell yet. I think we want to keep a tight hand—each of us on our own thoughts. I think at the present moment you are in a state of mind that hungers for the disaster it fears. If there are these forces of evil you see you are siding with them in allowing your thought to panic. Your mind is your own province—the only thing that is. Yes, this brings up another point. There is a sort of hubris in this unreal worrying. For if you have achieved peace in your own mind when the worst happens (if it does) you will have reserves of strength to meet it. And if you have not achieved peace in your own mind how can you expect the world to do any better. You are the world and so am I. And at the moment the world is a great deal too articulate! (You will agree!!) and worries too much and so on. My God—the hungry generation—ours appears to be famished. If you knew the letters I still get. The ones from the women—all so hungry and worrying. Hungry for a nostrum, a saviour, a leader, anything but to face up to themselves and the suspension of belief. I am thinking of one particular letter. I'd send it to you but I had my bag pinched the other day and the damned thing in it. It is sad for them. It is like a baby cutting its teeth and fighting against it all the time: 'Oh, what is to happen to me now, oh, these teeth. The future is nothing but one large tooth, oh, is there no saviour to save me from my tooth?' Yes, our times are difficult but our weapon

is not argument I think but silence and a sort of self-interest, observation and documentation (I was going to say not for publication but I am hardly in a position to say that!).

I shall love to come to your party on the 13th and shall look forward to seeing you then.

There is a P.S. thanking me for a book by Laura Riding:

> I agree with a lot of what she says (which must be a weight off her mind) but deprecate that turgid style. It is difficult for me to read here or anywhere just now. I seem to have lost the art—or shall we say any sort of matey interest in other people's thoughts. When music deserts me—it will no doubt come back. Thank you also for all you are doing for me about that review. Hope the *NS* proves more reasonable than *T & T*.

The next is dated '28 '38' and is on her nice yellow copy paper so she must have written it in the office. It goes:

> Here is a poem. I'm not absolutely sure I've remembered it rightly but it's something like this. And it is exactly how it happened. I also wrote another one but I haven't sent that because it has to have a drawing. There is a tall thin man pointing his finger walking in the desert and with him a lovey dovey sort of woman, all eyes and flicking eyelashes with pyramids in the background and an enormous solitaire diamond on her hand.

The poem which she sends is not as far as I can see in any of her books. I think it is very good and she may have left it out by mistake. It goes:

GOODNIGHT

Miriam and Horlick spend a great deal of time putting off going to bed.
This is the thought that came to me in my bedroom where they both were, and she said:
Horlick, look at Tuggers, he is getting quite excited in his head.

Tuggers was the dog. And he was getting excited. So.
Miriam had taken her stockings off and you know
Tuggers was getting excited licking her legs, slow, slow.

It's funny Tuggers should be so enthusiastic, said Horlick nastily,
It must be nice to be able to get so excited about nothing really,
Try a little higher up old chap, you're acting puppily.

I yawned. Miriam and Horlick said Goodnight
And went. It was 2 o'clock and Miriam was quite white
With sorrow. Very well then, Goodnight.

There is a quick handwritten letter about her publishing troubles:

> I am rushing this off in haste as I've heard today from the *Glasgow Herald*—so please don't bother unless you already have. Miss Donaldson has sent them all back to me as she's tried them on several of her colleagues and they all think they are 'too sophisticated'. It's they who are this not my poems, a sort of half-baked sophistication—I mean they can't see what anybody means unless it's said in the accepted voice. I now address myself to all old pards, including you love, as the great unaccepted. Truly I need a shover, a wee honey tongued worm to belly around for me, some pretty young man, eh? With a theory. Well, your old battle axe on the *New Statesman* won't have me, nor John Leighman [*sic*], nor Spender, nor Ian Somebody on *The Spectator*, nor Ackerley on *The Listener*. Only *Punch* will sometimes if they are funny. Love! love! And at my age it's tricky! I feel cross and send you a little poem I wrote because I really did enjoy Brighton. Best love to you, pet. And suffer these growls.
>
> STEVIE

With a line at the end: 'Oh, damn this Scotch one'.

I have two letters from May 1940, a bad bit of the war, in

one of which she explains that she has not persuaded her aunt to leave London and stay with a sister in the country: 'We agree that home is best and for travelling one must take one's chances, and anyway it is mostly underground.'

Six weeks later, after I had lost my baby, she writes:

> I imagine that the fact it would have been a horrible new world to grow up in is no sort of consolation and that those considerations, strong enough in theory, don't amount to much when it comes to it. I think it will be rather a horrible new world and a pretty hungry one too if we carry on the war as I have no doubt we shall. . . . But I am sure you don't want political chat so I will put a sock in it for it goes against the grain.

We must have met in London during the war for I was there a good deal on and off. But the next letters I have are not until the Fifties when she was much more of an established figure and newspaper or magazine editors were delighted to have her poems, and I hope some of the people who had turned her down before were a bit sorry they had!

III

You May Well Ask

WHY WRITE?

WHY DID WE want to write? What is all this compulsive story-telling about? I look at my shelf. More than a book a year since it began. Why? Is it simply the externalising in an increasingly skilled way, because of that pleasurable, of the stories and phantasies of childhood? In a sense yes, partly. Why, then, should we suppose that other people want to read these stories? Perhaps because story-telling has been part of the human environment for so long that we feel lost without stories. Writers have come to count on that.

How did it start? In my twenties I was having interesting, highly detailed dreams, which had only to be trimmed off and finished in order to turn into stories. One of these, for instance, was 'Niempsor Kar', which comes into *Barbarian Stories*. Another was 'The Hostages'.* And then there were the plays that I kept on writing. Dick read one and suggested it might have happened about the sixth century A.D. What was going on then? I had no idea, only I knew I hated history. He found me Volume IV of Gibbon, Bury's edition, which I read with great interest, forgetting it was history; I was twenty-one, just the age for Gibbon. But how did the situation come to be as it was in the first chapter of Volume IV? I must find out. I read backward through Gibbon. Then I read Mommsen. Then I was on the Cresta Run, no stopping.

Before that I had started two or three modern novels, but as I was completely without direct experience of the emotional or social situations I had got into my plots, they were very bad and the main characters were all versions of myself, a common

* Here I had originally made the boys Greek, but Theodore Wade Gery was so shocked at the idea of a Hellenic city being conquered by barbarian Romans, and indeed there is no example from the Greek colonies, that I changed them to Etruscans. Even so the story seems to me to lack genuine historicity.

enough fault in young writers. I began one or two modern plays but never finished one; but I saw things very much in dramatic terms or later in terms of movies.*

The Conquered, my first book, came out at white heat and, what is more, I wrote all the best bits, the juicy bits, first, all the bits that were most exciting and satisfying to write, like the very end. Then I filled in the rest, but I enjoyed that too. The beginning is really me and my brother, romanticised, in a Sennen background. But I was absorbing all kinds of experiences, turning them into a river to drive my mill. Once we were crossing the Channel, probably on the night boat to Dieppe; immediately the dark waves became the same as terrified Dith saw, two thousand years back.

There was a little garden between Cheyne Walk and the Embankment, already fairly full of traffic. Here I used to push the pram, for it was assumed that if one had a baby and a pram one had to push it. I had a big notebook, probably one of the Royal Commission ones which I had liberated from my father, and I used to have this opened out at my end of the pram so that I could write my book while I went on slowly pushing. No right-minded baby of course would have done anything but grab it, and from time to time I collided with other prams or people. Still, I got a good deal written this way.

I was uncertain, all the same. Perhaps I wasn't grown-up enough. I sent the MS to Rice Holmes, the historian whose rather dull book about ancient Britain I had read so meticulously. He sent it back with the comment that he could not possibly condone a book which had a chapter starting with a preposition (a deliberate 'And'). Professor Ernest Barker, however, was more encouraging and wrote me a Foreword. I read everything aloud to my mother, who was somewhat shocked at my chapter headings from *The Irish Volunteer* and *The Croppy Boy*, but otherwise gave me a nice warm feeling. In fact I read aloud to anyone who would listen; I still do.

* The first part of *The Corn King and the Spring Queen* was originally headed Reel One. It would of course make a smashing movie, but utterly unlike my own imaginings. Nor would I be playing the heroine.

The book went to John Murray, Sidgwick & Jackson, and certainly one other publisher, and came back; I wept and went on writing the stories in *When the Bough Breaks* and rewriting bits of *The Conquered*, incidentally taking out a chapter 1, which as I remember rather vaguely was unnecessary and historically wrong. When the novel was at last taken by Jonathan Cape I was terribly excited. They asked me to come and see them.

I bought a cloche hat with a tassel; it was made of patches of coloured leather and must have been fashionable. When I got to Bedford Square there were Jonathan Cape and Edward Garnett, both waiting for me. Me! Edward had expected me to be older, and look more like an historian. I felt very young. They asked me if I was Irish. But they were going to publish my book and the only thing they didn't like about it was my first title, *Headlong Westering*. This always happens; I had a struggle to keep *The Corn King and the Spring Queen*, later on. But nothing worried me that day. I went bounding out, hardly able to believe it, and ran all the way to Birrell & Garnett's bookshop in Tavistock Street to tell them the news. David Garnett was very sympathetic and listened while I poured it all out.

That was the beginning of a good publishing relationship which went on for more than ten years. Dear Jonathan had a certain tendency to fatherly pawings of his younger female authors, so I shifted when possible to Bob Wren Howard, nearer my own age and no bottom pincher. Edward Garnett was a marvellous adviser, who wisely made me think again about some of my early verse, and I wish I hadn't left the firm in a moment of anger with him, over the cuts they wanted in the name of decency in *We Have Been Warned*.*

The Conquered, published in 1923, was an almost immediate success. I was discovered by Raymond Mortimer. Oh how I lapped up the reviews! That first novel has echoes of Kipling. In later books there are echoes of D. H. Lawrence. But I was developing a style of my own. Oddly enough I was the first to see that one could write historical novels in a modern idiom: in

* See 'A Note on the Literary Decencies', p. 172 ff.

fact it was the only way I could write them. Now everybody does, so it is no longer interesting.

I got a great many letters about *The Conquered*. This is something writers need, and a phone call isn't the same; you can't pick it up and look at it again years later, when you are exhausted and unhappy. The reviewer in the *Times Literary Supplement* wrote to me. Perhaps the letter I was most moved by was a set of verses, clearly from someone at school, and unsigned. If he (she?) is still there, please write to me!

That book has been reprinted very often. In the last reprint I very much wanted to rewrite it to something nearer what I now think might be the real picture of a first-century B.C. Celtic civilisation, and to take out a few passages which strike me today as embarrassingly sentimental, though I so much enjoyed writing them. But the book is really by someone else. How can I interfere with her? It was some years before my books began to be written by *me*.

After *The Conquered* I got on to my Greek period, though always with occasional lapses back into Celtic or Saga country. It is odd to recollect how once I got started, various scholars and professional historians came willingly to my help, knowing that I would live into their period and make it more real to them. I did special things for them, like putting in the peacocks that Professor Adcock wanted. And there was the great romantic W. W. Tarn, who defended Alexander and Cleopatra against their more orthodox detractors and told me much about third-century B.C. Egypt. There was Arnold Toynbee—sometimes. And always there was H. T. Wade Gery, my main influence on the Hellenic world. Later I worked as a gentle critic with him and Maurice Bowra, who had been my brother's most brilliant New College undergraduate, on their Pindar translations, and Maurice was there when Wade Gery went suddenly out of my life and I felt that for me Hellas was finished.

I had not been to Greece when I wrote *Cloud Cuckoo Land*, but when I got there it was as I had intended it to be. Equally I had never been to the part of the Republic of South Africa which I describe in the first chapter of *A Life for Africa*; nor have I been in Outer Mongolia, described at length in *Solution Three*; I have imagined it from my elder daughter's description of life there, and I am sure it will be just like it ought to be if I ever get there.

It was the same with the cycle of plays I wrote in the Twenties which had a vaguely Byzantine background, but in which the main place was Marob on the shores of the Black Sea, somewhere to the north of the Danube delta, with a Graeco-Scythian culture. I first got involved with Marob in the sailing boat which took workers and guests out on expeditions from the Plymouth marine investigation station, where I was staying with Julian and Juliette Huxley. Marob came clear in my mind out of the bounding of the Channel waves off Plymouth, and comes, at various stages of its history, into almost all my books.

As far as possible, I took trouble to look at actual objects which might have been—just possibly—used by people in my historical books. Thus, whenever I see the beautiful British bronze and enamel shield in the British Museum, I feel it was once mine. In Oslo, not only could I see the Bronze Age gear, but I was allowed to have a splendid bronze torque on my own neck; only then did I realise that, like a Gladstone collar, a torque with its cutting end-spirals compels one to hold up one's head proudly, generating real living pride. Equally, the heavy bosses on a woman's girdle and her thick golden bracelets compel a certain attitude of the body which leads to attitudes in social life. Much later, in Copenhagen, I was shown and allowed to hold their precious copy of the Flattey Book with the meticulous, totally committed handwriting still exquisitely legible. And in the Hermitage Museum in Leningrad, in 1932,* I saw the marvellous objects from the kurgans which Berris Der made in *The Corn King*.

The same delight I had racing through London after *The Conquered* was accepted, the need to run, caught me at Cloan at the end of writing *Cloud Cuckoo Land*. I must have finished it late at night, for I gathered my typescript up early before it was

* See 'You May Well Ask', p. 188.

quite light and went out through the never-locked front door of the sleeping house into dawn. The Ochils behind us cut off the eastern light, but I ran uphill to meet the sun which had already illuminated the strath and the far range of the Highlands. In one of the high fields among bracken and wild pansies I met the sun, I plunged into light, I showed it my finished book.

But six years later, when I had finished *The Corn King and the Spring Queen*, I remember only feeling somewhat exhausted and not knowing what it was really about.* As it happens I have a complete time-sheet of that book, though not of any of the others which were usually fairly straightforward. I started it in 1925: 'London and Varengeville: Part One to the middle of Part Two.' After that I was mostly writing short stories and there were various external happenings like the General Strike. In 1928, 'summer to winter', I wrote in Spreacombe and London. Much of Part Three was written in London 'with bad cold just before Christmas'. This period also covered the illness and death of our son, which echoes somewhat throughout the book.

I then worked hard at it in 1929. The record goes: 'Winter London rest of Part Three. Working out Part Four. Spring Oslo and Stockholm Part Four.' (Here I also got a great deal from the Viking ships which went into short stories and also *The Swan's Road*, and later on *The Land the Ravens Found.*)

A note says 'Isobel as Archiröe'. I remember watching her face as we went by train to stay with her uncle Llewelyn Powys in Dorset and trying to describe her. I suddenly leant across the railway carriage and smacked her face so as to see what Archiröe would look like surprised and humiliated. But of course I explained afterwards.

After that: 'Whitsun train, weekend in Paris Part Five. Summer to autumn Cloan. Train: Paris. Train: Germany, Part Six. Autumn to winter London mostly Part Seven.' A note is

* The book went into several editions and got much praise. One letter about it that was very important to me was from H. G. Wells, who wrote: 'I think it is one of the greatest historical novels ever done. . . . I've got excited about it, lost in it. Erif Der, little Red Fire, is more real to me than most people I know. And I really believe it is something like what really was. Wonderful.'

'Elizabeth' (Harman, later Pakenham) 'as Metrotime'. 'Part Seven chapters 1, 2, 4 and beginning of 3.'

In 1930 'winter was in Cornwall' (I went down with the boys and read *Winnie the Pooh* in the evenings which we all enjoyed enormously). 'Chapters 3 and 5. January and February [1931] London Part Six and half Seven. Journey to Paris other half Seven. April Port Meirion Eight and Part Eight chapters 1 to 4. May London Part Seven chapter 5. June 11th and 12th. Oxford and London Epilogue.'

I remember quite well sitting at my desk, in the River Court drawing room, writing what I knew was the last paragraph of the book. On the floor to my right Lois and Avrion were building a tower of wooden blocks. With a bit of my mind I wondered which would happen first, the end of my book or the collapse of the tower. Exactly as I wrote the last word, down it came.

While I went on writing novels in the Thirties, Lewis Gielgud and I were collaborating over our plays. We always thought we might manage one which his brother John or his friends would like! Our method was to talk or write long letters all round the theme, and then get ourselves together in one place or another to spend four or five days all-out on the writing. When Lewis was in Paris with the International Red Cross, I used to cross by boat and train; at one time he had a very nice central flat and a charming North Korean refugee writer, Seu Ring Hai, who looked after us, but whose cooking—I often did the marketing, which I enjoyed—suffered from garlic in absolutely everything. He consulted us about going back to Korea: should it be, politically speaking, via New York or Moscow? After some hesitation we advised Moscow; one day he went off and we never heard from him again.

Lewis and I worked all evening until the exhaustion point, laughing like mad at our own jokes, I writing down the dialogue and then typing during Lewis's work hours. We would go to the local café or Chez Louise, where I occasionally danced with the lesbian professional ladies who came to eat and dance in congenial surroundings before they went to other bars to earn their living. Some had families to support. Louise herself was that way, with the barmaid as her wife. I remember once in the late Thirties going there with Margaret Cole; Louise thought I had at last seen the light.

The plays Lewis and I wrote, especially the historical ones, seemed to me to be competent, interesting and with the necessary suspense and tension; we were careful about the unities.* But they were not what was, apparently, wanted. One of them was done by some group, but we wanted the real thing. Anyhow, even though nothing came of it, this playwriting was enormous fun, and two of the plays were published. At this period almost anything I wrote was published and sold on my name and reputation.

In real terms of purchasing power I suppose I earned almost as much by my writing in the early Thirties as I do now. But there were more bookshops then and hardbacks were not thought of as a luxury, to come long after drink, food, tobacco or clothes. While I was writing *Cloud Cuckoo Land* and later *The Corn King*, which overlapped the birth of two children and the death of one, there was a continuous spin-off of stories, poems, biography, children's stories and occasional articles. I also did regular novel reviewing for a time, convenient when nursing babies. If the books were not very good, I could manage two at a feed, one for each side, though as the babies got old enough to realise I was not paying total attention, they would get annoyed, let go and protest, or bite.

I read French almost as fast as English, and in the early Thirties did reviewing of current French novels for *Time and Tide*, which was then in full flood, with a number of good authors writing for it. It was the first avowedly feminist literary journal with any class, in some ways ahead of its time. Lady Rhondda was always tremendously encouraging and gave gorgeous parties. I remember

* I had never forgotten the lesson learnt years before from G. B. Shaw, to whom I had sent some of my earliest plays; he had rebuked me for showing 'a glorious disregard' of the unities, and went on: 'You will find, if you study the most effective modern plays, that they are the ones in which the unities are most closely observed, even at a considerable straining of the device of coincidence by which all the persons of the play turn up miraculously in the same place at the same moment.'

driving back from one of them, cautiously since there had been a fair consumption of alcohol, but feeling splendid, as though the whole world was opening up and everything would work out, not only for myself, but for women in general.

I was also involved with *The Realist*, a journal, monthly I think, started with immense energy and publicity by a highly impressive editorial board of which I was much the youngest. Arnold Bennett was chairman, but there were also Sir Richard Gregory of *Nature*, Julian Huxley, Eileen Power, Malinowski, my brother, H. G. Wells and Rebecca West, Gerald Heard and various others. The object was to bring together the three worlds of art, science and the academic humanities. Old copies are still impressive, with their good paper, nice margins and pleasant print.

Arnold Bennett was extremely kind to me, though he teased me a little, as when he demanded that I, then in a Republican mood, must be the one to propose the Loyal Toast. *The Realist* was financed, at the start, by Lord Melchett whom we met before or over an excellent dinner. My job was to find promising young poets; I found Auden. But by that time rocks were in sight; I was one of the few who asked questions about the financial side. Lord Melchett's secretary was somewhat annoyed; so was I when he referred to me as 'another of those Huxleys'. But when we pressed for an answer about when the next cheque was due, I recollect his phrase about his employer: 'Poor Lord Melchett, he has such a bad memory.'

I know there was one more slap-up dinner before *The Realist* folded. Gregory sang *Mademoiselle from Armentières* and I was just a bit shocked though I pretended not to be. But I was now observing the secretary closely, as I wanted him as a model for one of the Alexandrian baddies in *The Corn King*. I liked to watch him telling lies and he found this very annoying. People don't like being watched obviously and professionally. Once, on a more intimate occasion, someone threw me across a room for this.

In the middle of the 1931 general election, Victor Gollancz asked me to edit the *Outline for Boys and Girls*. This was something new, but fitting in splendidly with my political preoccupations. Yes, I would do it and an impressive lot of authors I collected, among them Hugh Gaitskell, Wystan Auden, Margaret Cole, Gerald Heard, Delisle Burns, Olaf Stapledon, Clough Williams-Ellis, N. W. Pirie, Professor Winifred Cullis, Beryl de Zoete and Richard Hughes (oddly enough writing at his own request on physics and mathematics). It was extremely hard work; one had to bully, cajole, alter to the extent of almost complete rewriting, fuss over, flirt with or accept doubtfully one's authors. But we were very hopeful. The book was clearly needed at that time.

It should have been a success and Victor was good at gauging successes. But the *Outline* was torpedoed by a vicious attack from Arnold Lunn on behalf of the Church. I can't now remember in which prestigious paper it came out, but it was effective on other reviewers and sales. What were we to do? Unfortunately it was Yom Kippur and Victor was unavailable; between one religion and another I fought for my book and my authors and, on the whole, lost.

I gained, however, in friendships, especially among the scientists. Winifred Cullis was a great encourager of positive feminism; I got to know both Piries, who stood so splendidly by Denny later on at Cambridge. And I also got somewhat entangled with John Pilley, then teaching at Bristol University and on the edge of the Communist Party, which at that time had its intellectual members, well able to make poor old social democrats feel inferior. He helped me a lot with the actual science editing.

Collaboration with Dick Crossman on the life of Socrates was less successful. He was then at New College and I thought he was bullying his students; we had words about it, which spread to our writing. However it is the only time I ever stole a car, even temporarily. People didn't lock in those days, and I abducted a parked car from outside New College and drove Dick and his then loved one to Wytham woods where they could see one another safely; I then drove them back and re-parked the car. I wonder if the owner ever discovered it had been missing.

About now I began to plan a sociological book, a description of some of the worst bits of British slum life. I knew Birmingham more or less, but now went to Leeds, one or two other Midland towns and Glasgow where the slopes at the back of the City Hall, now smartly built over with modern office blocks, had ancient single-ends off a twisting stair, all in solidest stone. The M.O. who took me round told me to keep my hat on as 'they' were apt to fall off the ceilings. In one of my diaries, I have noted a few remarks from the people I talked to (with details of their rent), for instance: 'Don't know when it was, the last time I had a bath, couldn't tell you in God's truth.' 'It's wicked, it is, makes you feel sick, it does'—the smell of bugs. Or just this from a woman, 'Never go out nowhere' and from another, 'No pleasure'. But I never got this book much further; it was too big for me, in the time I had to give to it.

At one period, too, I started writing a book about feminism. I read around the subject a great deal. I find beginnings, notes and possible plans for it. But this too never got off the ground.

And the shadow was beginning to fall, Hitler over Europe. It comes into all my books of the late Thirties, especially *The Moral Basis of Politics*, which I hurried over, feeling it was essential for social democrats to have strong rocks to hold to in the hurricane; and again it is all there in *The Blood of the Martyrs*, published in 1939 and swept away.

A Note on the Literary Decencies

Not so long ago my books were thought of as a possible menace to the respectable reader. It is funny to think that I was generally considered to be near the verge of obscenity, a writer of real bed-time books, although I never used or would have been allowed to use, a four-letter word. Still, I managed all right without them.

The lines that were drawn seem very curious now. Clearly, I no more understood them by ladylike instinct than I had understood the lines of conduct I was supposed to keep to earlier, as a teenager. My letters from Edward Garnett, Cape's reader, all of which I have kept, go back to 1925 when apparently there was a 'slight alteration of two or three words' probably in *Cloud Cuckoo Land*. He writes, 'A great many people are not in our happy position of taking sexual facts simply and naturally and they might raise an outcry, which would be annoying.'

In 1928 he writes: 'I stuck up for the "poor bloody tarts" verse and told Cape that there was an indirect relation between it and the story, but Cape is a puritan and he said it would cost you and him a couple of hundred readers!! In future you should take a stronger line and tell him that you insist on the inclusion of a piece. Don't bow your neck in the House of Rimmon.' This was in fact a poem which I had written for *Black Sparta*, but it wasn't particularly good except for some nice internal rhyming which I was keen on at the time. I ended by substituting another, and better, one.

In 1929 Edward writes: 'If Cape worries you about changing passages in *Barbarian Stories* I should simply refuse except in the matter of two or three isolated words. I am suspected of being on the side of licence against the Law and Commerce. So I have no influence to help you but only to harm you by espousing your side. I simply advise you to stick to your guns.' He used to come to tea at River Court and talk, always helpfully and with an undertone of—not flirtation, but the warm relationship between male and female which can be very valuable to both. Clearly he liked *The Corn King and the Spring Queen*: 'It's frightfully interesting and audacious and full of brimming life and high spirits.'

I had a spot of trouble with that book where at one point I had actually dared a four-letter word. I didn't think I'd get away with it, nor did I, though my substitution was fully as clear. But *We Have Been Warned* ran into much more serious trouble. There is a seduction, a rape, much intimate marital chat, an abortion scene in the Soviet Union (straight from the diary of my visit there in 1932) and so on. Not overmuch in a long book. But it was too much for Jonathan Cape.

And here Edward Garnett was no longer on my side, which was very upsetting. He had liked my early books so much, but he clearly disliked this book and was disappointed that I had written it. He wanted a great deal cut, what he calls 'loose superfluous stuff. The author's pen seems to run on, putting down all that occurs to her and there's an over-fluency about many other passages that makes them inartistic and very often tiring.'

When it comes to the various sexual episodes he is even more in disagreement and clearly finds a great deal of it full of 'acute emotional sentimentality'. In another letter he says 'it has suddenly struck me that you would strengthen your novel a good deal if you cut out most of that sexual stuff in the Russian part between Dione and Donald and Tom and the Russian girl.' Some bits had definitely shocked him, especially anything about contraceptives: I don't suppose any reputable writer before my time had mentioned the unpleasantness of the touch of rubber.

Edward had been reading my Russian diary and says firmly how much better it is than the novel. He may well have been right there but the general idea of asking for a complete re-write was not acceptable. I have a copy of my letter back to him saying:

> I am sorry you don't like the book but I was afraid you wouldn't. Perhaps it's inevitable. I'll consider your criticisms but in general I am afraid I can't accept them. You see, I am more sure about this book than I've ever been about any of the other books. I know Dione behaves in an odd way but I am quite certain of her behaviour. She isn't a completely normal person any more than Erif Der was or than I am myself. Possibly I am suffering from a complex of sexual obsessions myself—I expect many people would say so.

And then about the scene he specially didn't like between Dione and Idris:

> Don't you see I've got to make that scene as beastly as possible (a) to offset the Russian scene and (b) to get Dione's reaction afterwards? I've cut and altered the book a good deal already.

But a lot of what you don't like is stuff that I worked over a lot, read aloud and so on; I know it's not what it ought to be on a lot of grounds but I must finally go my own way. I'm awfully sorry because as you know I've always taken your criticism before and always believed in it. You are my literary godfather. But I've got to do this on my own. After all I am thirty-six and I must be able to judge for myself.

There is now a series of letters throughout summer and early autumn of 1933. They start off with a list of the words and phrases which he wanted to have altered and I have a copy of my letter back. Here I keep asking at the page numbers: 'what's wrong?' or 'what on earth is wrong?' Over one I protest: 'This is all written with immense care and I am extremely reluctant to alter it. You will see that I have carefully left out all the taboo words and there is no kind of description of sexual organs. It is written as carefully as verse and everyone who has read it says it is beautiful.' In one passage I have allowed some substitution and cutting, saying: 'this shortens it and I think should satisfy people'. In another passage describing a studio party I say, 'What exactly is wrong? Is it "a poet and some boyfriends"? Surely that passes? Or is it "a little lovenest from the BBC"? I could ask Joe Ackerley and Gerald Heard if they minded! I think it was them I saw that night. But I am willing to substitute if it worries you!' In another passage I make allowances and say 'substitute fun for fucking'. But it didn't go far enough and the correspondence continues.

The next letter is from Jonathan Cape very much in person saying about one scene, 'I am not at all sure that the printer would not decline to print it even then. It would be altogether better if you were to rewrite it and modify its tone very completely.' And again: 'The whole of this scene is highly dangerous and it is a question whether any printer would print it. Pages 326 . . . and on to page 327 would lead inevitably to police seizing the book and its destruction. The whole scene is open to objection and puts a most deadly weapon into the hands of your orthodox opponents. It will need to be rewritten and drastically recast.'

There are various other things. Even the adjective 'bloody' appears to be too much for him. He ends, 'If you will follow these recommendations and modify the passages in a thoroughgoing manner—these suggestions are the minimum—I think the book may get through.'

Among the sentences which Cape didn't like were these from the part of the book which is set in the Soviet Union: 'She had brought these contraceptive things for herself and Tom: it seemed somehow indecent to use them for herself and Donald. She was cross with herself for thinking that, but the thought remained. And if they failed.' Again, 'She found a dirty shirt and smelt it tentatively; yes, this was how he smelt. What did she think of it? Nice, not nice? She didn't know, she couldn't make up her mind even about something as easy as that. She couldn't this evening be sure of anything in the world.' It seems to me now very curious that those two passages which seem to me to show a normal feminine sensibility, were thought to be obscene.

In a later scene with Donald and the Russian woman the cuts included: 'Her hands were now on his trouser buttons—he couldn't let a woman do that! "I do this, comrade," she said. He let her.' Other phrases which had to go include 'with her legs open'. In the book she says, 'You got—rubber goods—comrade?' Cape wanted rubber goods out and again, very oddly, I was allowed to write of her soft breasts but not, as I wrote, 'breasts and belly and legs'. Again, later in the book I was told to take out 'without any of those damned silly ineffective rubber goods'. Clearly this was one of the main areas of contention. Again in the rape scene, a phrase I had to take out was 'his elbow off her nipple, his hot legs and body off her'.

The argument went on and on. I finally write in September:

> So now I am asking you formally whether you will or will not take this novel? I cannot agree to the extensive alterations that you think necessary, though as you know I am willing to make certain small alterations. If you decline to take it then

> I am afraid that you must regard yourselves as having refused the book and I cannot agree to any restrictions being made on my offering it elsewhere. As regards my next book after this I cannot remember any clause about it but will look at my contract when I get back.

All this meant a real break and I was very miserable about it, especially about the hurt to my long friendship with Edward Garnett. But before I took the book completely away from Cape in the spring, Jonathan Cape sent me some alternatives which I still have and which are just much poorer than my own original versions. In one I was told I could keep the word 'button' if I omitted the word 'trouser'! I just felt I wasn't going to be bullied. By that time too we were not even in agreement over terms.

I then sent *We Have Been Warned* to Victor Gollancz, the obvious publisher for a left-wing book. He writes a quite reasonable letter, dated 17 July 1933, which does I think show the climate of opinion at that time:

> My dear Naomi,
>
> To put the main point first I am not going to make you an offer for the novel.
>
> This decision is the result of thinking round the thing very carefully in the light of (a) a report from a man to whose opinion I attach a good deal of importance, (b) a report from and a discussion with Sheila Lynd whose reaction is important as being typical of a body of young but not reactionary opinion, (c) discussion with Ruth who has read all of it. My own opinion (with which Ruth's by the way independently and exactly coincides) remains quite unchanged. While there are points here and there which I should have wished to discuss with you I think the thing as a whole is quite magnificent. It is I believe the first piece of genuinely social art (using the term as parallel with proletarian art and as opposed to art for art's sake) that has been done in England in our time and I believe it to be immensely valuable as such—the sexual parts no less

than the political and economic. It makes me feel ashamed of publishing almost every other novel that I have published. But it is absolutely clear to me as a result of reports and conversations that bits of it (and bits which in my view should not be changed) will horrify an overwhelming proportion even of people who would otherwise be sympathetic, and that publication of the book would cause a real outcry.

The two things that have been working in me against my immense desire to publish the book have been (1) a shrinking before the certainty of jeers and abuse from many of my best friends, (2) the fear that my efficiency as a publisher of socialist books would be seriously damaged by my association with the publication of a book which will undoubtedly be widely described as 'filthy'.

As you know, there is nothing harder than to be honest with oneself in these things and I cannot be sure that I am being honest when I say that I think I have squashed the first of these difficulties and that it is only the second which is operating. Still I do think so: I think that is to say that if it were simply a matter of being jeered at by most of the people I like best I should quite happily face this. . . .

I tried the book on John Lane and they too turned it down. Then I sent it to Constable who said they would take it as it was; they put it into page proof and then started querying. I still think this was a dirty trick for any publisher to play on an author and I wrote back telling them so:

The whole thing is extraordinarily disappointing. You see I specially asked you about the decencies before we agreed on publishing. I asked you about this particular passage. It is crucial for the book and has already been toned down as much as it will stand.

I told you that Cape wouldn't take the book because of this question of decencies. If I had been willing to castrate the passage in question he would of course have published it this time last year. But I was not willing—hence the fact

> that you got the book. And never say you weren't warned. . . .
>
> Every bookstall in England and America—yes, in every country except Russia—is full of magazines which are calculated to throw men and some women into a state of sexual excitement. Anything can be said if it is said in a sufficiently dirty and underhand way. And I am not to be allowed to print a piece of honest and straightforward love-making! I wish you'd had it as I first wrote it, then I could have 'toned it down' to this and you would probably have passed it. If I had been less straightforward myself I would have done so. I wish I had.

I go on: 'Of course I myself would be delighted to have a good row. There is nothing I enjoy so much as controversy. I would not compromise at all if I had not to think of my husband's political career and the mud that's likely to be thrown. Mud's not going to hurt me—but the Tory papers are infinitely malicious and they might hurt him.'

I was extremely upset about all this. I have quite a number of letters from other people, including a very understanding letter from Michael Roberts, who saw the book as quite different from anything I had done before on a subject where the end could not be seen but one must reach out into the future. He writes: 'It's like a first novel, you've used far more material than you can master. You can afford to drop some of it (e.g. the reference to the feel of rubber in the skating instructor scene: it's good and exact therefore it will annoy. Don't let them confuse the issue by something like that: you can say all that next time).' And then:

> Don't bother to be too insistently explicit: the great thing is to get the stuff accepted by its public and then bit by bit force them to realise its implications. . . . Publish this book as your publishers wish: you'll hate taking out anything, it will seem that all the best has gone but there's more good stuff in it than you remember. And it's all true. That is the way some of us feel about things. (Incidentally it's a woman's

book, there's no attempt to pretend you've a man's mind, a mind tending to rationalise at all sorts of comic moments.)

I must have told him about the disapproval of Labour Party stalwarts. 'What's the good of people who've been in the movement twenty years? A pretty fine mess they've made—the world still at the mercy of newspaper and armament magnates and definitely with its back to socialism! Don't listen to their whimpering and their assumption that being in the movement is a way of life. It isn't, it's a means to an end.'

I think probably Michael was right but by this time I had got into such a jam that I simply couldn't go back and do all this rewriting. If I had taken his advice and cut the book even more drastically than the publishers wanted, but followed it up with something harder hitting, I might have made more social impact. But I didn't. Instead, I went back to writing historical fiction.

In some of the stories in *The Delicate Fire* there is, I would have thought, far more overt sex than in *We Have Been Warned*, but apparently it's all right when people wear wolfskins and togas. This book and *The Blood of the Martyrs* probably had a political impact on some people. But by the late Thirties people were more hardened over sex, bloodshed, torture, death and all that.

However, I have uncovered a fan letter, I think dating from 1939, which reads:

> Having just read *We Have Been Warned* I write to inform you that of the thousands of books I have read it is far the filthiest. In spite of the foreword one can only suppose it represents the views and modes of life of socialist and communist 'comrades'. Apparently murder, perjury, drunkenness, foul language and moral depravity of every sort are their stock in trade. I wonder that Constable published it. I suppose it was a bit too thick for 'Comrade Gollancz'.

Well, well, there speaks the soul of the Conservative Party. Or doesn't it?

My next modern novel was a Highland comedy, *Lobsters on the Agenda*, in which the word 'bloody', by then as familiar as breathing, was sprinkled through the dialogue in a normal way, and in which the doctor, interrogating someone on whether he had got a girl pregnant, asked questions which might have shocked Jonathan Cape twenty years before. But by then nobody noticed.

But what are we writers doing, with all this compulsive story-telling? It is like a spell, something laid on us and when we stop being able to do it, presumably we have lost the way; we die. It is well for me to remember that some writers went on to my age and beyond, not at their most typical but sometimes at their best, like the later Kipling in his short stories. It is deeply uncomfortable to have periods of not being able to write, when we become desperately afraid that the magic whatever-it-is has deserted us. It is also somewhat uncomfortable to be in a real writing mood, but to have to do all the other things that people with homes and families and responsibilities have to do. But the writing will probably keep, the exact words will slip back like mice into a darkened room.

That doesn't answer why we do it. Nor is it an answer simply to say: Because I want to. Alas, as one gets older, there are fewer other pleasures: delight is imagined rather than experienced. The body is no longer a pleasure-giver; we have to be wary of it. Only the tick of the story-telling goes on. Only the words, appearing and offering themselves.

There is no doubt a certain economic pressure, growing as sterling wavers down. There is pride in a skilled job—what else can I do equally well? All skills are pleasurable, but we must stick to our own. Not long ago I tried to make a pot, even a small bowl, on a potter's wheel; it looked so easy, so delightful, the flowing clay moulding itself precisely where the fingers of the potter wanted it. Not at all. The lump of clay leapt up and landed all over me.

Yet surely anyone can write, at least an accurate description of something they have seen? But no, no. This is why it can be faintly irritating when someone says 'Oh, I could write a real good book if I had the time'. Try, my friends, try. It's not so easy. Many people can't even make an omelette or fry a herring decently in oatmeal. Which leaves the main question—why write?—unanswered.

YOU MAY WELL ASK

MUCH OF THE above leads back to politics. You may well ask how people like us—and there were a good many—came to call ourselves socialists and to join the Labour Party but without altering our way of life very much. We did alter it to some extent but we still took holidays, still had a big house with a staff to run it as we expected them to do, still gave parties, were still recognisably ourselves.

The end of World War I left us not in a state of eagerness for change as we were to be after the Second War, but knocked flat. We were all beginning under our breath to blame the older generation. They were the ones who didn't realise why we needed the League of Nations; they and their friends the generals had sent our friends to death. But there seemed to be so few of us left.

However, a kindly neighbour just a few doors along Cheyne Walk but in a house twice the size of ours, Lady Courtney, Beatrice Webb's sister, called and invited me to tea; probably she had been asked to do so by my Aunt Bay. The price was to join the Women's International League, but that was all right, though I didn't pay very much attention to the issues which, as far as I remember, were at first mostly about averting some of the worst consequences of the Treaty of Versailles, though there was also some feminism about them. We signed petitions and sent resolutions to our MP. But alas, what I remember most clearly was being told by Lady Courtney to move a vote of thanks to a speech through whose entire argument I had slept (probably having had a baby-broken night). Gallantly I leapt to my feet and said that nobody could have enjoyed it as much as I did.

Even then I knew at the back of my mind that if I got really involved with politics it would be exceedingly bad for my writing. If I thought too much about what was going on in India or Israel

I would cease to be able to concentrate on what was going on in Rome or Hellas at a considerably earlier date. I had been deeply moved about Ireland, partly by Yeats's poems, but without political understanding; it only seemed to be a situation which fitted in with and illuminated Caesar's conquest of Gaul. But the first political procession I marched in had *Peace with Ireland* banners, and I was with Margery Spring Rice. Gradually we came to know more and more of the Spring Rices' circle, keen and knowledgeable liberals mostly, and the time came when we dined and spent the evening together two or three times a week, talking politics and the arts and of course children.

My Uncle Richard—Haldane of Cloan—had advised Dick to go into Liberal politics. He would have helped. Later on Dick wished he had taken this advice, but he wanted to get on at the Bar first. Yet the pull was towards Liberalism and, for me, early feminism. When it came to the General Strike in 1926 neither Dick nor I was clear about where we stood. I suppose we might both have felt at home in some conciliatory group. But we did not really know what it was about. My father certainly supported the Samuel Report but probably did not go so far as totally to support the miners. I at least was more worried about the children than anything else and also somewhat envious of our strike-breaking friends who were doing gorgeous things like driving real trains.

In the late Twenties I began to read quite diligently, feeling I ought to. I got stuck early on in *Capital*, but felt I must struggle along, half a page, half a page, half a page onward. Yet it was all rather remote, not only from my comfortable London life but still more from fifth-century Athens or wherever else my imagination happened to be.

Dick, however, was beginning to take it all very seriously. This was largely due to the Coles, whom we had known for a long time. Probably Douglas Cole both as teacher and writer had more influence over the younger left-wing intelligentsia than anyone else at this period. Margaret was the moving spirit of the Fabian Society. They also collaborated on one detective novel a year. We began to see more and more of them, to share holidays, to talk and discuss. Yet I scarcely contributed to the arguments; my mind had as usual wandered off on its own. Then came the time when Douglas, who was Parliamentary Labour candidate for King's Norton in Warwickshire, was discovered to have diabetes. Dick took his place almost immediately before the 1931 general election.

From then on King's Norton—a hopeless seat as the electoral boundaries then were—became the most obsessive part of our lives. Our first election agent was Arthur Davis, but after that for years it was our dear friend Tom Baxter and his wife from a Labour Quaker family. In the middle of the campaign I joined the Labour Party, convinced not so much by the arguments as by our new friends. When Tom talked about his time at the mines it all suddenly came real to me, and he was lovely to dance with. There were others, among them Len Edwards, Harold Nash, Sid Hines, Leon Thompson, Mrs Cook, Frank and Thea Griffiths; their faces or voices come up momentarily as I write their names. I found it immensely moving to be among them, accepted and loved because of our common cause. This was the beginnings of the Thirties recession with the respectable economic slogan *Step Down All*—too bad for those at the bottom of the ladder—so that I could see it in intellectually easy terms of justice as fairness.

Probably most Parliamentary candidates' wives, moving into a constituency, are going to find themselves among people fairly like themselves with the same tastes, prejudices and incomes. If they are at all good at social know-how they will easily get to understand who can be trusted and where to drop in for a useful chat and hints. It wasn't like that for me. I was very uncertain and made social blunders and misjudgements. I could not at once take to the Midland voices, still less the usual standards of taste. Sometimes no doubt I was insufferably patronising; often I failed to see the real problem, assuming it was to do with personal relationships when it was really to do with money, or the lack of it.

But gradually I got to know King's Norton better, staying with people and visiting in a non-political way, though I don't suppose I ever got to know the really poor, the lumpenproletariat, in any genuine sense. But, for the others, the social barriers gradually broke between me and the gentle Midlanders whom Douglas Cole accused of having chocolate-coated souls. (It was half true: many of our people worked at Cadbury's in what were, for the time, unusually good conditions with not unsympathetic employers.) There was a deep layer of respectability; I had not worn my wedding ring before, on feminist grounds, but Tom said I must wear it now. And, only too often, a hat. Our handsome friend Rudi Messel stood for Aston, a real old slum constituency in those days. A dear Midland lady asked if he wasn't a film star. I said, 'No, a Labour candidate.' She said, 'Oh, only that!' But then remembered herself and approved.

Harold Laski came down and said, 'You just press a button and I make a speech.' My brother came too; his great gesture to demonstrate a point was to slap his thigh, but he sometimes missed. George Lansbury came, though not, I think, to that first election. Once I watched him carefully while he made one of those marvellously moving speeches; he would glance at his watch and then shift key, carrying us with him: it was all worked out and why not. Afterwards men and women in the audience crowded round just to touch his coat sleeve and to feel comfort and refreshment. That had nothing to do with rational economic argument.

I can't really tell what Dick was like as a speaker. The candidate, like the sacrificed king, must be built up by all, most of course by his wife, who must sit there with an interested look and lead the laughter at the jokes, however often she has heard them. I couldn't speak myself unless I wrote it all out beforehand—not till later I listened to all the speeches at the public meetings and helped with committee-room work, though I never could get to like committee-room tea. At first I was very shy about canvassing, but at Fircroft, where we stayed, I made constant omelettes and coffee and saw that we always had slabs of chocolate. At the end of the election campaign I went to the count and tried to comfort our people who had worked so hard, and yet in a way I was already looking forward to going back to River Court and my own writing and the small children.

General elections without telly, and with radio not very competently used, were more fun and more local; one saw much less of the national leaders, which was perhaps a good thing, especially for those of us in the audience who were acutely counter-suggestible. We often had big meetings, though the smaller ones in the further-out corners were often good value. People wanted them and the eve-of-the-poll meetings were full of shouting and enjoyment, rushing the candidate from one to the next. We were all worked up and there were plenty of scraps, though nothing to match the crowd violence of modern football. In '34, I think, we had a rather small man driving us around in our beribboned car; as we stopped somewhere I saw a chap on a motorbike drive up, apparently to attack the driver. I intervened and, somewhat accidentally, hit him on the point of the jaw; he went over like a tree. I was terribly upset as I had supposed myself to be a pacifist, and my arm ached afterwards, either from moral guilt or the force of the blow. Anyhow the man picked himself up and after that always waved to us cheerfully from his bike!

At King's Norton I always wrote a Message to the Women Voters, usually with photograph of self and baby; it was rather shaming and one had to do it with half one's mind shut. Some of my writing must have seemed a bit phoney to many people, though oversimplification and loud shouting are part of the election fight pattern; it seemed to have gone down all right, probably because it was at bottom a kind of love. And I was able to help Dick, who found this type of writing hard, though he could draft a Bill or write anything completely realistic and sensible. Printing was not expensive and we always had Election Specials with rhymes and jokes as well as serious shorts, and lots of different posters; no doubt Dick contributed in cash whatever a candidate was allowed, but certainly no more. I think this would have been true of all the better-off Labour candidates, and nobody tried to cheat.

I got to know Birmingham, which is Sallington in *We Have Been Warned* (Marshbrook Bridge is King's Norton), and I wrote about it again in *The Fourth Pig*. The whole ambience of those early election campaigns is caught, I think, very well in the Sallington chapters. Tom, the candidate-hero, is somewhat

Bennite. But surely Dick was too? One would say so, from the political proposals and carefully-worked-out Acts of Parliament in his book, *The First Workers' Government*, published in 1935. If there is really such a thing as 'left', Dick was probably on the left of the party. Perhaps then, as now, there were the inevitable stresses between the socialist intellectuals and the solider, more experienced trade union leaders. Naturally I saw it all almost wholly from Dick's side of things, but even then I could not help feeling that jealousies came into it.

After a few years of King's Norton, I started to write a book: *Kitch against Caroline*, in which I used conversations, including phone calls, for complete chapters: old hat now. I also had a working committee which was to keep me right on detail and help with the probabilities of the story. We had some fascinating meetings. In my novel, Kitch (short for Kitchener) was a draughtsman. I got the class and skill differences rather well sorted out and my committee were keen and vocal and often usefully critical. Then, after the 1935 election, Dick decided to move to a winnable constituency. I said goodbye to my committee with tears and kisses. I couldn't go on with the book alone. Besides, events were catching it up and making nonsense of the main political plot, which included a revolutionary situation in the United Kingdom.

Events in the world outside were also moving on. In 1932 I went to the Soviet Union with the Fabian Society party. Before we set off we all met for a kind of briefing from Beatrice Webb. Much the least experienced of the group, I sat waiting to hear what the others, including my cousin Graeme Haldane, would say. Suddenly Beatrice turned on me: 'What is your field of investigation?' Much alarmed, I stammered out: 'Archaeology and abortion.' Two A's. I had certainly been thinking of looking at museums and getting down to the Black Sea country I had written about, and seeing what was happening to cultural activities marginal to the five-year plan, and I also thought I should ask about family planning; but now I had slipped and would have to go through with it, or the priestess would disapprove.

And so I did. As Intourist or whoever was organising things got it into their heads that Graeme and I were brother and sister and could conveniently share a room, I also got in some engineering, including a fascinating visit to the great dam of Dnieperstroy (where they threw stones at us). I described the abortion which I rather reluctantly saw in *We Have Been Warned.* But the archaeology was wholly delightful, and the book-length diary I kept of the trip has excellent portraits of some of my fellow voyagers: Pethick Lawrence, Weldon and Opie, Kitty Muggeridge, Christina Foyle, with whom I shared a cabin, fascinated by her careful make-up and hair-do, above all my cousin Graeme, by that time a top electrical engineer, constantly trying to see power stations and ask technical questions and only too often foiled by bumbling or suspicious officials. It was clearly a profound emotional experience, not only for me, but for most of the people who started off from Tower Bridge, across the North Sea, along the Kiel canal 'in the sweet and heavy smell of hay', and on to Leningrad, whether they were members of the SSIP* party or others, enquirers or devotees.

I was critical as well: 'a lot of Sparta about all this'. But, apart from a few officials, I clearly loved all the people I met, including the incompetent but friendly guides of those early days. The words that I keep on using are 'gentle', 'kind', 'helpful'. I met a good many people and had long discussions on such topics as the interpretation of dialectical materialism as applied to archaeology and how the daemon flourishes in different ways at different epochs. One museum archaeologist showed me one of his pieces, saying, 'Ah, you will have seen this lion at the exhibition, but you will not have touched him: caress him now!' So I did; he was a delicious bronze lion with a grin.

Investigating archaeology involved great difficulties with Intourist, who didn't want stray visitors dangling off to Kerch. I had to change trains at one station, so I sat on a bench with my typewriter on my knee and wrote my diary; a great crowd collected. I demonstrated what my *malinko machina* would do, but the stupid thing wouldn't write Russian letters. The police

* i.e. Society for Socialist Inquiry and Propaganda.

came and shut its case, for by then the crowd was well over the railway line, and we all laughed—my sole brush with the GPU.

The diary records my journey through the Crimea with Professor Marti: driving in an ancient landau over the steppe brilliant with flowers and lark song, feeling the early Slavonic or Hellenistic coins and objects in the museum at Kerch surround me as I slept there, and somehow communicating with dear Marti in dog Latin. On the train back to Kerch, after exploring the kurgans, we were both soaked with sweat in the Crimean heat:

> Marti began to talk to the man beside him, a factory worker, explaining that I was an English socialist. Then they talked politics and then archaeology. The man brought out some coins, a Finnish one and a Turkish one. Then the man next to me who had been listening reached over with a coin out of his purse, a very fine big bronze coin or token of Nero which he had found here. Marti read the reverse but was puzzled by the obverse. I made out most of it (it was a Pax Terrae Marique) and he confirmed it after borrowing the first man's spectacles and then he gave the carriage a little lecture about Nero, which they loved. They all asked questions. I got the feeling that Marti was on the best kind of terms with these people; each —worker and archaeologist—respected the special qualities of the other but were equal as *people*. That's so utterly right. They were very friendly to me particularly when I read the inscription (which made me feel a little less ashamed of myself for having been described as a *working* archaeologist by Marti). They had the most sympathetic and good faces, something open about all of them. I kept on wondering whether people's faces are really at all different between classes in any country. We are conditioned to think so (that so and so looks like 'an English gentleman') but I don't believe they are. Certain kinds of beauty seem to be produced by one class and others in another perhaps; but in general we judge by externals, by clothes, by accent in England (but how difficult to tell with foreigners!) though this becomes less marked with the

influence of the wireless and with one's own growing distaste for university English and by manners, though these approximate more and more nearly too, as sensible parents begin to insist less on external manners for their children and allow them for instance to eat as though they really liked eating as the children who have gone hungry really eat.

Some of these workers had very fine faces and usually calm ones, though they expressed their emotions. At the end of the journey the second man took back his bronze coin, looked at it and then shoved it into Marti's hands. 'For the museum.' Of course he really felt it was his museum too!

Here is another vignette from the Crimea:

I swam out and saw under me in the very clear water a fine-looking pillar lost from the city. Then a girl joined me who turned out to be my friend's daughter; she spoke good French. She is a physicist in Leningrad and was very beautiful. She was really terrified of war with other countries—it was obviously her nightmare: to see all the new lovely socialist things they had been building up destroyed by the awful people with teeth and claws and money and swastikas like on the posters. She asked me as we sat in the sun drying whether people in England didn't hate Russia and want to destroy it; I said I thought very few people wanted that and only because they were frightened and that many people were full of sympathy and goodwill. I do hope that's true; I believe it is. . . . I asked her if she is going to have children and she said 'Yes, yes, I have one now', looking with pride down on her beautiful golden brown body just softening a little into the new curves. She said she was very well and had all she needed; her husband is a physicist too in the Leningrad Optical Institute; she seemed to me an extremely good sort of person. For a time she and I played about with a large jellyfish and then dried and dressed.

On the way back into Western Europe I opened my suitcase

and said to the customs man: 'That is my diary—do you want to read it?' He, however, had spotted a splendid Russian doll: 'For whom?' 'For my daughter, Lois.' 'She is how many years?—Ah, I have a daughter just so old!' Exchange of photos, with diary and other papers not even glanced at.

The paper of the diary is dry and brown and brittle. The first and last pages are gone. Like me it nears its end. These quotations perhaps give the flavour. I was not converted, all the same. They were them, I was I. Still, the visit left me, like many of us more or less left-wing socialists who had read our Marx and all that, with a somewhat ambivalent feeling about the Communist Party. This comes out clearly in *We Have Been Warned.*

Yet it was difficult for most people in the Labour Party, at any rate the non-trade unionists, to regard the CP as the real enemy. Somehow we always hoped that history might take a different turn this time: hence the United Front with Stafford Cripps trying to build durable bridges in the late Thirties. Neither Margaret Cole nor any of the politically minded Postgates and their main allies could regard the Communist Party itself without suspicion, though they knew and liked so many of them. I was in two minds, partly because of my brother. He was for some years a card-carrying Party member, assuaging no doubt the guilt of being born into the upper classes; this doubtless increased the tension between him and me, since I had not sufficiently recognised my guilt. He certainly tried to cut luxuries out of his life, except for the spiritual luxury of open quarrelling with our mother, something I almost always avoided but sometimes still dream of. But his other strong loyalties cut, perhaps painfully, across the political one. For instance in the Thirties he began (I believe) to write a life of our father, whom he was so proud of and loved so deeply in spite of their political differences. Later, whenever I asked about it, he flared into anger.

But what did we well-off middle- or upper-class men and women in the Labour Party think the end product of our socialist thinking and planning was going to be? What were we after and what future did we imagine 'after the revolution' in the sense at least of a revolution being a turning upside-down of society? Some were in it because they saw the breakdown of capitalism coming and wanted an alternative. But I, more romantically, saw it as a moral issue, justice as fairness. Above all I felt that in a fairer world people would become automatically nicer, all social intercourse would be happier and easier.

Like most of my generation I was deeply influenced by William Morris and the idea of everyone working part of the time with their hands, making things—of course with unerring good taste!—and all eating together from piled pottery bowls of salad and fruit and wooden platters of cheese and meat set out on oak tables. If you had put it that way I would have laughed and taken a tough attitude, but I certainly believed that economic liberation would bring with it all kinds of other liberations; political change was never envisaged as a boring redistribution, not only of wealth but of other standards.

Morris's *News from Nowhere* envisages a post-revolution world in which only the goodies make the running and apparently all wounds are healed. Morris had not been near a revolution himself. We have been and we know it is not like that. But did we believe that a socialist society would mean a complete destruction of our kind of life, as clearly a revolution with any reality ought to have done? Not really. That kind of belief is very, very difficult to hold for more than a few minutes, especially if you have children: hostages. We would certainly have agreed that change was necessary, was admirable, but we went on planning for things to go on as they were going. So did a good many other people who realised that the economic system was not only unjust and internationally dangerous but very likely to break up through its own contradictions. Likely perhaps, but the system was more flexible than it appeared to be and the old process of muddling through continued.

Meanwhile we were beginning to live in a background of fear at the thought of what the next war might be like. We were all much influenced by the pacifist arguments, especially perhaps Aldous Huxley's *Ends and Means*. We felt that wars were always made by capitalists, especially by the 'merchants of death' for their own profit. We distrusted the military mind. Many of us had experienced propagandist lies during the last war and we didn't intend to be taken in again. King and Country no longer had any appeal. We disliked our government intensely. But neither Dick nor I realised that perhaps the only chance of avoiding war but containing fascism was to listen to Ivan Maisky, the Soviet Ambassador, and ally ourselves firmly, if not for ever, with the USSR.

I got to know Agnes Maisky quite well. There was often cheerful and vigorous Russian folk dancing at the Embassy parties. We noticed the English trade union crowd, who also sopped up the vodka, sitting on the floor so as to get a better leg show. Once in the garden there was round dancing that we could all join in and Ivan Maisky swept six-year-old Valentine up on to his shoulders to join the bounding, joyful dance.

The attack by the Dollfuss government on socialist Vienna in February 1934 was, I suppose, the first of the series of hideous civil wars we are living through, forerunner of Spain. The Austrian Chancellor, Dollfuss, no doubt under pressure, attempted, for a time successfully, to make Austria into a corporate state, as Mussolini had done with Italy. The first step, the liquidation of 'Red Vienna' where a socialist municipality had done great things for the workers, is documented in my *Vienna Diary*, published by Victor Gollancz in 1934.

What I did not, naturally, write there was that my main love affair had ended. My lover was now married and it had become increasingly clear that this was not compatible with his relationship with me. Lying on beech leaves under bare January boughs I had asked, 'Is this the edge of the precipice?' He answered, 'I am afraid so.' The moral imperative said I must agree, not only verbally, but with everything in me. In the novels of an earlier period deserted heroes used to go and shoot bears in the Rockies; I answered a long-distance telephone call from a left-wing friend, quickly collected money including a generous advance from Gollancz, went off to Vienna and was tolerably successful in forgetting my wounds, at least for a time.

Looking back on that time, what I remember is the constant

feeling that I was deeply one of the Second, Social Democrat, International, a European in brotherhood with European socialists: *Freundschaft und Freiheit*, we whispered to one another in the hurrying, anxious streets. I doubt if the practice of infiltration by the opponents had yet got very far. There were still decencies to be appealed to and sometimes admitted by the other side. In fact when I look back at my book, what astonishes me is the mildness of the 'atrocities' which upset me and all of us so much, and the general amiability of the police. The sides have hardened since then.

We ourselves were heartened by the slogans, and the chalked-up three arrows—is it used still? We worked till exhaustion, but there were moments of shattering beauty—an afternoon off when I went to the great picture gallery and saw the Breughels, their attitudes of despair in face of cruelty, the same as those of the persecuted socialists in the Gemeinde houses. Or again dodging the Leoben police by walking across a small pass to a branch line and the sight of the gentians in the Alpine meadows. There were strange alliances, between socialists and Nazis—decent enough men, like the governor of Leoben prison with whom I had a curious conversation, each of us being quite open as to our political opinions, perhaps slightly hoping to convert the other. I asked him if I might see one of his prisoners, Paula Wallisch, widow of the hanged socialist leader Koloman Wallisch, and see her alone. After a little hesitation he agreed and himself called back the warders so that Paula and I could talk.

In the latter part of the time my main companions and allies were Evert Barger and a young Welshman whom I called Glyndwr in my diary. What fun Elwyn Jones, now Lord Chancellor, had, telephoning back in Welsh, not then understood by the Austrian police! Hugh Gaitskell, our other comrade, was at his best. He and I had a rather unfortunate flirtation earlier on and had left one another angrily, but this made up for it. We were constantly having to keep in touch and warn one another. Once I had to warn Hugh that the police were being rather inquisitive. He would be coming home by a certain large square; I must wait for him there. Oh the embarrassment for a well-brought-up young woman, having to hang around in a Viennese square!

Yet when I look back my clearest memory is of crouching in a corner of the stone staircase going up to the top flats (no lifts) of one of the Gemeinde houses, a socialist girl comrade with me and the noise of the feet of the Heimwehr coming up on a search. They would certainly have arrested us; probably I would have been let out at once but she might have had a bad time. A mouse running across just as they came: *Ein Mauserl!* They went past us laughing. I remember getting terribly disheartened and then something would happen to cheer us up, some act of courage and generosity. The Austrian women comrades laughed at me for getting nervous and anxious, tough cookies who had been through a lot and expected to go through more.

I think it was in Vienna that I had lunch with a nice young Englishman called Philby; no doubt we talked politics. Betty Lascelles, an old friend, was in the Communist Party, but the British Embassy at long last took notice of what was happening when she—with her surname!—was arrested. Then there were Gedye and Voigt, both first-rate newspapermen in their very different ways. Dear Gedye and his great dog Strupye! He gave us all his suits for the refugees we were getting away across the frontier, to make them look more like respectable tourists.

One thing I left out at the end of my work, for the sake of other couriers, was that I was carrying papers from socialist friends to their British comrades in my thick woollen knickers, across the Austrian frontier. I had practised walking with them, but it wasn't easy. How relieved I was not to be effectively searched. But probably one's enemies are much more efficient and less gentlemanly now.

Denny's school, Abbotsholme, had an exchange arrangement with a German school, on the lines of Gordonstoun. The German school had started to Nazify in a highbrow way, probably calling it character-building and not perhaps giving a glance at that vulgar young Hitler, though it would all come to the same thing in the long run. Denny, who in his late teens became a very serious Young Communist, painted red hammers and sickles on various doors and bolted. I met him in Paris, looking really remarkably dirty even for one of my children, and we went to visit some old revolutionary—which? He had assassinated someone, no doubt deservedly, and Denny was thrilled.

Up to this time public speaking had been somewhat of a nightmare to me. I could just stumble along if I had it all written out, but even that was very difficult. But I came back from Vienna; the train drew in to Victoria. Dick met me and said, 'There's a Fabian Society meeting this evening. I know you hate speaking, but give us ten minutes on what happened.' I answered, 'Ten minutes? I shall speak for an hour!' And so I did, with no difficulty, for it was all there, bottled up, waiting to burst out. I spoke afterwards at all sorts of meetings, including big halls where I had to use a mike though, Haldane-fashion, I preferred shouting. And after that I never had any bother, though I like public speaking less now.

Sometime in the Thirties we attempted to make a propaganda film to show at Labour socials, a worthy object for they were apt to be extremely dull. It was Rudi Messel's idea and he got together the equipment and organised the shooting, some of which was done in the open at Hammersmith. The old bridge on the creek was very photogenic. A few scenes were shot in George Lansbury's house in Poplar, and G.L. looked in on us from time to time, mildly amused at the goings-on of the young. I was the mother of the young man on the dole and had to remember between shots which tooth to black out. But it came to nothing in the end and just as well, for it was simply one of the old acting games in an ideological sheepskin.

But there were others apart from our constituency friends who gave us a real insight into how things were and what capitalism did to people. I got to know Walter Greenwood in the early Thirties, about the time *Love on the Dole* was published and when he was still very firmly in that world of industrial Salford about which he writes. He never, even in his years of prosperity, quite lost the look of it. He was always thin and pale with jutting bones and wavy brittle hair. It was as though he had never been outside a Lowry townscape.

At first he was very shy with me, but he got over it. He had got a small advance from Cape for his book—I think I did a bit of prodding there—but it was all used up. He wrote when he was waiting for the next advance:

> . . . the weekly crisis, E's home getting into rent arrears through sickness of the eldest boy. Is it to be wondered that she looks old? We nearly fought again last night . . . still, I've only to look at that old coat of hers to understand. Poor lass, she has not had anything new for two years. . . . *Time and Tide* paid the three guineas but I touched my agent for a fiver so I still owe him the difference. I'll get this I think from *Labour* next month. I loathe debts and obligations of any kind. . . .

He went on worrying about contracts on and off in all his letters. But of course it mattered desperately and sometimes he thought back to even worse times. In one letter:

> I'll never forget the awful misery of 1931–2 when E's other bloke, who had a nice regular job and who wanted to settle down, was competing with your then unemployed, ragged backsided boyfriend who had the unwritten *Love on the Dole* on his chest and a manuscript that regularly came back and who didn't want to settle down in a two up and two down 'two children, the rest birth controlled'. I felt awfully defeatist. And I've not yet got the poison out of me.

He was writing hard and also kept on his old job as a clothing club collector which would bring in a small weekly wage. But Labour politics were the main thing and he fixed up with the Salford agent, 'a taciturn, careful, guarded bloke', to get Dick over to speak at a meeting. Getting speakers for a meeting mattered in those pre-telly days. Several of Walter's letters refer to meetings and what happened. Clearly Dick's was a great success. There was another early in 1934 at the Manchester Free Trade Hall with Tom Mann and Harry Pollitt and an audience of 4,000:

> The CP locals can give us lessons in the technique of collecting. Their plan is first to say how much they require from the audience. On Sunday it was £60. Then the chairman asked for ten £1 notes, nor did he stop asking until he got them: then twenty 10-shilling notes that also were forthcoming: then forty 5-shillings. Then the ordinary collection was taken. The result, £63 (accepted cheques and IOUs). We'll have to rehearse one of the King's Norton chairmen. Speeches were so-so: fire-eating on Pollitt's part and jibes at Stafford: 'One minute he is shaking his fist at the King, the next he is down on his knees asking God to bless him' (or words to that effect). Some derisive laughter. One thing about the Communists is that they don't conceal the way they mean to get what they want if the chance comes. But what does annoy me is that they claim a monopoly of revolutionists and revolutionary ideas. . . .

He goes on, 'I still think our only hope is Dick Mitchison's shirt-sleeved fighting policy. If the Labour Party fail next time it'll be their end. So it's up to us all.'

The first time I met Nehru was at King's Norton during the election campaign of 1934. He had come over there to see something of English politics and was the guest of the Quakers. Dick and I were both very much worked up, kept moving around fiddling with things. What was so extraordinary about Nehru was his beautiful calm. Clearly he was in sympathy with us, but it came out in the smile and the look; his voice was never raised, nor his hands. Later, I was asked to arrange a get-together for Nehru and Stafford Cripps, so I gave a dinner party. I was not very sure what Nehru ate, though naturally one would keep off unseemly beef. But on the morning of the party Stafford's secretary rang up to say, 'You know Sir Stafford only eats things raw.' Finally I arranged two of the big silver salvers handsomely with salad and raw vegetables grated or sliced, but also cold chicken and salmon. I had made splendid dishes of piled fruit on the table between the candles, which everyone grabbed for. The other guests included Julian Huxley and my brother, two of the most arrogant people around at that time. They scored off one another happily and the critical talk between the politicians continued in a low key.

When in 1935 it appeared that there was no chance of a Labour win at King's Norton, Dick moved to a new constituency: Elland and Brighouse. But I took against Yorkshire, their insistence on contradicting me forcibly whenever possible and various other minor matters. I missed the Midlanders, to whom I had said goodbye so sadly.

In the late winter of 1935 I made another political journey, to America, with Zita Baker, later Dick Crossman's wife. Our return tickets cost £26 each on an American cargo boat which took a few passengers. I made a scrapbook of cuttings and photographs and poems, but it is now with the Southern Tenant Farmers' Union, of which I am a member. How come? Well, when we got to New York—after a voyage of ten days and landfall at Boston in the snow—I had introductions to various people including the socialist leader Norman Thomas. He sent us on to Professor Amberson in Memphis, Tennessee.

We had bought a second-hand Ford; people said we should take guns, but we said no, no, they might go off. Well, they said, at least never give lifts. This too we disregarded and we gave lifts to all sorts of delightful people, white and black, some of whom helped us to put our car together again when bits fell off it, while others sang to us.

In time we got to Memphis and, through Professor Amberson, Zita and I got involved with the sharecroppers in the black soil, one-crop, cotton country the far side of the Mississippi. At that time—not yet having, for instance, seen Howrah or the Palestinian refugees camps—I had never met such poverty: the houses built of old pieces of tin and cardboard, the children obviously suffering from pellagra, American children who didn't know a chocolate bar when they saw one; poor whites and poor blacks living equally badly and determined to struggle together for a slightly fairer share of the cake and also perhaps for *Freundschaft und Freiheit*. We went to packed meetings in candle-lit rooms with boarded windows in case there was shooting. It was very early spring and there was always an open stove in the middle into which all spat after chewing. Very few had socks. I told my friends about the Tolpuddle martyrs, and then about Vienna and comradely solidarity. I was asked to speak at the open-air meetings; the custom was to begin every speech with a Bible quote, of which there are plenty applicable. I had no trouble with this, but my poor chairman at one meeting had bad trouble, for he put his hand on my shoulder introducing me: I was a white woman, he a black man. Someone duly shot into his house, but luckily he was warned and under the bed.

Zita and I, both being personable young women, were good publicity for the sharecroppers. The Scripps-Howard chain of papers sent sympathetic reporters who gave us space and photographs. Would we, asked the chairman, head the march to Marked Tree, the administrative centre? If we did there would be no attack. We said Yes of course, not taking this seriously, we with our good British passports. But there were the two wicked sheriffs, like characters in a movie, leaning against the walls, one at each side, and spitting across our road! However, they desisted and we led in the march.

Zita was a splendid person to be with, ready to join in anything and everything; we usually shared a room and I was only sad when I found that she didn't believe my true accounts of the preceding night's dreams. She told me rightly, I think, that it was time I started wearing a bra, which I had not done so far. We went to Taos and stayed with Mabel Dodge and Tony Luhan in a lovely adobe house with a hand-potted clay fireplace where the crackling piñon branches heated our room deliciously before we got up. There was marvellous dancing; I longed to join but clearly it was for men only and of deep ritual importance. When one of them dropped a feather from his splendid gear I made to pick it up, but Tony held my hand back. If I touched it the man who dropped it would have had to go through a long and painful penance.

From Taos we went on to New Orleans where we met with lots of nice, leftish students. I wanted to go for walks but kept on coming to dark inlets of water that I couldn't cross. Anyhow they thought we were crazy to want to walk instead of riding in someone's car. We decided we must go to Washington and tell those in power about the sharecroppers, and we got some advice on whom to lobby, but found, on the whole, worse than indifference. Nobody wanted to know or hear. At last I said: 'There's only one thing to do: we must send a straight account and the photographs we took to Roosevelt; they just might get through.' That was what we did. We got no more than a formal acknowledgement. But the legislation which began to change things for the better, starting the sharecroppers on the road out of deepest poverty, came a few months afterwards. Perhaps we helped a little.

It was sometime after that that I joined up with Mass Observation. This was due to Tom Harrisson, whom I met first in his young days, when he was an undergraduate beginning to rebel against the accepted norms in a way that became more usual twenty years later. Nobody had yet invented the terms 'hippie', 'drop-out' and all that. Not that Tom Harrisson dropped; he jumped very hard and the bottom came out—as he intended it to. I tried to help this young man, sometimes wondering if it was worthwhile. It was.

He started by jumping on respectable liberalist semi-academic Oxford in a booklet *Letter to Oxford*; here he pulled to pieces various Ox-attitudes. It seems very mild now as compared with today's attacks on accepted social mores by the various protesters, but it raised a considerable storm at the time. It didn't worry me, I was outside by that time and had done my small bit to axe the Ox. But doubtless it made it harder for Tom to get academic backing for his projects.

Tom was black-haired, shaggy, thin and tough. He was deeply interested in people, which officially made him an anthropologist. He had a respectable South England background but that didn't seem to incommode him. He went about in sandals, a normal thing to do, one would think, but not in those days, not in Oxford, not for a young man who might hope to lecture and be taken seriously by academics. Once when he was in extremely good spirits, before going off on an expedition to the Pacific islands, I painted his toenails red.

The expedition came back and most relapsed into Ox-attitudes but Tom now wanted above all to investigate the people of Britain. This was the start of Mass Observation which grew tremendously both in organisation and in respect during the later Thirties and involved teams of volunteers, cross-class and cross-age. Mass Observation had no official support, as Tom indicated in a letter, undated but written presumably in the mid-Thirties, from Bolton where much of the anthropological work went on:

> I wish to God you could lead me to someone who would give me £1,000. The organisation is now splendid and constantly expanding. We are on the edge of major results. And we are utterly bankrupt, it will be difficult for me to find the money to reach London. To see the Labour Party spending £50,000 on propaganda without the first bloody idea of what they are doing keeps me awake with intellectual diarrhoea. It will be pure hell if I have to disband this show. Of course I can easily carry on myself working in any job and observing as I go. It's all v. worry making. I expect it will work out.

In a sense it did work out, mostly through the enthusiasm of a number of people very few of whom were professional anthropologists, but some of whom were involved with politics in one form or another. There were monthly directives to all the Mass Observers, some quite odd: What have you in your medicine cupboard? What have you on your mantelpiece? A mass of material has been collected (and is now housed at Sussex University) all due originally to Tom Harrisson, turning up suddenly, full of ideas, never afraid as the rest of us were, giving us back the confidence we would need in 1938.

I had not forgotten my old allegiance to the League of Nations idea. Over Manchuria I had expected action. Yet what could it have been? The League had no power, no army, no sanctions that worked, nothing. Except of course the hopes and loyalties of a number of intelligent but equally powerless people, the stage army of the good. After Manchuria it was Abyssinia (not yet commonly called Ethiopia). We detested Mussolini and all he stood for,* but what was the use? And by now events in Spain were boiling up, with that same Mussolini befriending Franco.

The Spanish civil war was like a wound on Europe. People we knew went out and some of them got killed. Surely the socialist government would defeat the rebels. But it went on and on. My brother went as an observer and expert in home-made bombs. At one point he urged me to go as a nurse but what would have been the use, for a month or so? I knew no Spanish. His stepson Ronnie went with parental encouragement and came back safe. I remember the Spanish fraternal delegate La Pasionaria speaking to the Labour Party conference in Edinburgh, cheered and cheered by almost weeping comrades. She must have thought it meant something. Well, so it did, but not the kind of support she needed and hoped for.

Sometimes International Brigade men turned up, possibly sent by Jack. I gave them tea and cakes. Once one of them asked if he could take off his boots. I proceeded to wash his feet, to his pleasure but also embarrassment. I however was back in one of my books, being Beric in *Blood of the Martyrs.* Everything comes in useful!

In spite, however, of my preoccupation with early Christianity (or perhaps because of it) my anti-clericalism grew. Once Jack and I both went to a Rationalist Press Association dinner. The chairman, Mr Whale, gave an impassioned anti-God speech fervently applauded and was then laid out with a sudden heart attack, round which all was agitated quiet, except for my brother's loud stage whisper: 'Harpooned!'

In 1935 I was asked to stand as Labour candidate for the Scottish Universities; there were still University seats in those

* My poem about D. J. A. M. Melly, head of the British ambulance unit, who died of wounds in Addis Ababa on 5 May 1936, the day Mussolini marched in as conqueror, begins: 'We are ashamed for Europe . . .'

days and they were sometimes held or fought by men or women slightly out of the straight party lines, so they had their uses. I asked, 'Shall I be elected?'

'No.'

'Shall I lose my deposit?'

'No.'

'Okay, I'll stand.'

Coutts' Bank, when I drew out my deposit, were discreetly friendly and encouraging. Arthur Woodburn was my agent but was rather upset when I wrote my own election address and wouldn't let him alter it or put in bits of Labour Party officialese.

It was a most enjoyable time. I liked Aberdeen best: the almost white nights of midsummer reminding me of Leningrad, the far side of that northern sea. I had crowded and enthusiastic meetings at all the universities and here I began to get the feeling that I was indeed a Scot and that Scottish nationalism had some meaning. But unhappily few of the audience or questioners were the actual voters; these stayed cosily away and on the day automatically voted Conservative. Still, I didn't lose my deposit.

I went to the Labour Party conference in the autumn of 1938 as the delegate of the Argyll Constituency Labour Party; possibly I was the only member who could afford the trip. They couldn't have paid anyone's expenses. Nor did they give me any directions on voting, but they knew I was a Crippsite and were duly impressed by my report when I came back. The conference was all rather remote from Argyll, the problems of the fishermen and small farmers or the unemployed of Campbeltown, where the original fourteen distilleries had been 'rationalised' into two and there was little else in the pipe-line. This was the conference at which Stafford Cripps was thrown out of the Labour Party. I voted for him, holding up my card with 1 on it. I happened to be sitting next to a large trade union, which sat on him like an elephant. That rising growl: 'Card vote, card vote!' Impossible to feel brotherhood with them.

Outside it was wet and windy and we walked up and down a very unpleasant sea front and along a pier and back, trying to encourage Stafford; this must have been Morecambe, marginally less nasty than Blackpool. I even said I would—and did—pray for him. He was terribly upset and for all of us it seemed to bring Hitler nearer, though I'm not quite sure why.

Was the Labour movement being desperately insular, burying its head in the sands of trade union disputes? We were, however, in touch with socialists of our own kind in other countries. If, for instance, we went over to France to see old friends again—but Dick's comrades of World War One were getting rather old—we found a lively militancy:

> Monsieur Laval avait promis
> De faire baisser le prix de la vie:
> La vie s'est enrichée,
> Laval s'est dégonflé!
>
> Ah ça ira, ça ira, ça ira,
> Tous les fascistes a la lanterne,
> Ah ça ira, ça ira, ça ira,
> ON LES PENDRA!

And so on, naming not a few politicians. Was there more political liveliness in Europe then?

During the later Thirties one of the happy things was our friendship with Nye Bevan. He was one of the warmest possible people, totally unlike his image in the Tory press. He never even had it in for us that we were intellectuals. He and Jennie had a gorgeous wedding party. Through the Coles, mostly, we got to know many more socialists, both from this country and elsewhere.

Looking back on it all, what is so strange and striking was the feeling we all had that, if we tried hard enough, the millennium—the revolution or whatever we called it—would come into being. Where there was a choice the signposts were clear. We knew which side we were on. Moreover, we felt we had a cause worth living for, even worth dying for.

Perhaps it is helpful to remember the good things that have come to our civilisation and especially to our own country and would not have come without the efforts and choices of the men and women of the left, as well as many who would not have called themselves political, especially scientists, doctors and engineers. I think of the general structure of the Welfare State and especially the National Health Service with all its shortcomings and difficulties and inevitable delays and unfairnesses, which the same kind of people try to iron out today. Few of my readers will know poverty as it was half a century ago. As people's expectations go up the poverty line goes up too. In terms of health there are so few people now dying of poverty diseases or crippled by them from birth that the more fortunate are seriously concerned. The disadvantaged and miserable have become news. They weren't news then.

And what about my own life as a political person? Would the world have lost anything if I hadn't made these journeys and had these doubtless mind-stretching adventures? If I had stayed at home and really studied local problems of politics, education and administration? If I had ever finished my own broken education? Or if I'd been a whole-time mother with perhaps more children? Or less?—but that's something I can't bear to contemplate. No, I just don't know. We go with the wave of our time, getting whatever is to be got out of it.

IV

Storm Warning

DEATH

THERE WAS NEVER a year when we were not in Scotland for a few weeks anyhow. While my grandmother was still alive we went up to Cloan as by right and I proudly showed Granniema my babies. She was by now bedridden but looked impressive, sometimes beautiful, with her long silvery plaits and delicate Shetland lace shawls. I still raided the fruit, but rather more openly, and still climbed Craigrossie and found parsley fern at the foot of the dark screes. We hunted for blaeberries. I wrote stories and poems. We even went swimming in the cold waters of the dam just up the glen and I would recognise rocks and pools that were part of my childhood's story world. Granniema sometimes told me stories about my forebears or about her own childhood, and it occurs to me that she may have wanted to see what I would swallow. Being someone who never clearly notices the gap between fact and imagination, I always found belief easy and pleasurable.

But Granniema was ageing. Her hundredth birthday, with letters and telegrams, was an occasion for celebration and family arrangements. But another occasion was coming. For a few years after 1918 we had been able to forget death just round the corner. Then it reasserted itself. Granniema, probably bored with her bedridden life, made various arrangements for her funeral and died. I went north. It was very much an occasion, with Cloan filled with flowers so that the scent of the lilies drowned the voice of the minister. I knew she would want colour so I brought irises and roses. Her coffin was taken down to the station in one of the red-wheeled farm wagons. She had chosen her team of horses but most people followed in cars or on foot at the pace of the Clydesdales. The old Auchterarder station was by now shut down, so we went down and up and over the long ridge of Auchterarder past houses and shops darkened and shuttered in mourning and men standing bareheaded to watch her go by, so to Gleneagles station which we still thought of as Crieff Junction. It was well kept in those days, with paint and flowers and the station master coming to meet the family and what they had with them.

My father was at that time much absorbed in the problems of heat exchange. Like the rest of us, he enjoyed working in trains and he wanted to discuss it with my brother who was also there. I had a poem in my head about the funeral, which I wanted to write down. Everyone was wearing funeral gear and my father's problem was that somehow he had acquired the wrong size of top hat, while doubtless someone else was struggling with his. I had a problem too as I had borrowed a black coat from someone (I hated wearing black) but it had a blue lining so I had to clutch it from time to time. In Edinburgh, where we arrived at the old Caledonian station, the traffic was held up on the Lothian Road and all descendants took a rope of the coffin, including Elsie and me, though I think Aunt Bay was too shaken. Perhaps she was the only one wholly grieving—it was her life that had completely shattered and was not yet re-forming.

Edinburgh friends and relatives had joined the crowd which followed after Granniema's coffin and her children and grand-children, to the graveyard across the Lothian Road. There must have been photographers from *The Scotsman.* Certainly there was the complete ritual and again flowers upon flowers. There is something to be said for all this. In Scottish culture nothing beats a good-going funeral. It takes the mind off other things, though my father's mind was definitely on heat engines almost all the time.

Uncle Richard was next. He had diabetes and as yet it had not been brought under control. I did not go to that; it was too near the death of our own son.

My father went to Cloan still and I usually took the children up for a visit at least. The place had become rather less formal, and Aunt Bay was always welcoming. I walked up the glen with the older boys, showing them my special places, but the woods had changed, some cut down, others replanted. The family rheumatism and sundry aches, called in those days sciatica and lumbago, had got at my father, though it was somewhat eased by up to ten aspirins a day—with no bad side-effects. We went for walks, but slower. Twice I went with him to Glasgow, once to one of his own Gifford Lectures, and again when he was part of someone else's audience and I was instructed to dig him in the ribs when he was too obviously asleep.

But in 1936 it was clear that his turn was coming. His lungs had never fully recovered from the effects of the work on poison gas during World War I. He also caught whooping cough later on from one of my boys, which didn't help. Then he did the thing which is so usual among the ageing—fell out of bed and could not get up. It was a high old-fashioned bed in his small room. Pneumonia followed. My mother meanwhile was laid out with a bad attack of cystitis. Today both would have been treated with antibiotics and the patients would have rapidly recovered.

I came down quickly from London. Fever was developing and my father much interested in his curious dreams. My brother followed a day or so later when it was clear that affairs were taking a bad turn. The doctors were devoted. It was no problem to get nurses. I managed to get my mother up and across to his room just once to see him. I remember how delighted he was, greeting her with words of love. He was much interested in his treatment, talking it over with the doctors as long as he could, particularly pleased when his temperature went down to a record low. But it became evident that he would not live. I thought he should be told but my brother refused. Next he was in an oxygen tent.

About now I think what happened was that I told some newspaper which enquired that yes, my father was seriously ill. At any rate I think this was the occasion for a bitter quarrel between Jack and me in the Cherwell dining room, though it could have been something else, but whatever it was became expressed by Jack in furious Marxist ideological terms. We could only quarrel in whispers because we were immediately under my father's bedroom; behind Jack's shoulder the bronze horses on the mantelpiece remained unmoving. I bit his arm; he twisted my wrist. Crazy unhappiness made us not care. Finally we broke apart and went soberly up to the sick room.

Dick came down from London; my father was very fond of him and the nurses preferred him to be the one to help them; he was steadier than Jack and me. My father died in the oxygen tent at exactly midnight. He had a look of intense interest on his face as though he were taking part in some crucial experiment in physiology which had to be carefully monitored. Jack and I watched him, one on each side. We could only go on the look, however much we longed to ask him. But it made me at least feel that here was an experience deeply worth having; I hope my brother was equally alert and interested and that I shall be when the time comes.

After it was all over, my mother told and various arrangements discussed and made, I got to bed in the small hours. The telephone went around seven in the morning. I staggered down to answer it, blear-eyed. It was, I think, the *Express* asking, among other things, how much money my father had left. This struck me as so bloody awful that I gave the poor chap on the night desk or whoever it was the edge of my tongue and he collapsed. But I knew it wasn't his fault and felt almost sorry for him.

The Radcliffe, to which my father had left his body for dissection, asked not to have to do it. They were his pupils and friends. They could not bear it. In the end he was cremated at a kind of non-religious service we had devised with readings from one of his own books and from the *Phaedo*. Aunt Bay was there, deeply sad. We were to take the ashes up to Cloan and scatter them. I remember the scene at Euston. Aunt Bay and I had first-class sleepers; it had been an exhausting time for me and she was no longer young. But Jack, clutching the parcel with the ashes, was determined to go up in an ordinary third-class carriage with the parcel on the rack. We were told what was what about the capitalist class travelling first. I suggested that he and I should swap on the grounds that he could more comfortably write whatever scientific paper he was in the middle of writing. Perhaps that would be acceptable. But it was no good; he wanted it the other way.

At the tiny graveyard by the old chapel at Gleneagles we found, predictably, a crowd gathered for a last honouring of the Doctor. It was a beautiful day. They sang *I to the hills*, as so many years later, in 1970, the boatloads at Carradale sang for Dick. Fair enough; we had not succumbed to religious orthodoxy, but allowed ourselves a little traditional comfort from our fellows.

Poor Maya, my mother, was still not well. She became very depressed and did some rather unnecessary shutting down of Cherwell. Perhaps as a symbol she sold the big dining-room table where so many guests had sat. But she recovered and became somewhat more herself, living through considerable difficulties with great courage and cheerfulness, especially when her granddaughters started their Oxford careers.

The links were snapping between me and Cloan. Aunt Bay died at the end of 1937. There was rather less of a crowd at the same family graveyard in the mouth of the glen, but more perhaps who had known her well and worked with her. Probably she would have lived longer had she been willing to be less active. But no Haldane likes sitting down and taking things easy. Her death was the end of something that mattered to me; I was sad for myself as well as her. She left me some money, not much, because she never had much of her own. I felt I ought to share it with Jack, perhaps stupidly, hoping this might heal the breach. But he gave it all to the Communist Party. I never quite got over that slap in the face.

Dick's father, to whom he was much attached, died while we were away on holiday somewhere by the sea in Brittany. The telegram came and Dick left immediately, but did not want me or the children to follow at once. My father-in-law's heart had failed, unobtrusively, as he had lived. Dick's mother died not long after. But there is less of a sense of occasion in English funerals than in Scottish ones.

Now only Uncle Willie was left, hoping to die on the hillside among the cattle, deliberately getting among the lively young Angus bulls. But, in the end, many years later, he had to put up with weeks of indoors, bed, nurses, and all that he had wanted to avoid before he could escape.

STORM WARNING

WE DID NOT deliberately consider moving out of London. Dick, in the normal course of things, would have had many more years at the Bar. My friends, my professional life, were London based. So was all the political manœuvring. Nor did we think very seriously that London was bound to be the main target area, although we had offered River Court as an auxiliary hospital, supposing a scheme for ambulance boats on the Thames had come to anything. But it all seemed too impossible to face: something was bound to happen to stop it, surely? The refugees from Nazi Germany and Czechoslovakia who crowded increasingly into River Court, having fierce ideological quarrels in the dining room, hitting the mahogany table with their fists and neglecting their good English bacon and eggs, forcing me to gather up all my German and shout at them to stop—these people thought otherwise, but then, who listens to refugees?

We had gone to Scotland, but not to Cloan, for holidays two or three times in the Thirties, rather against my inclination since it meant housekeeping for me. But Dick had become more interested in fishing and shooting, and so, to some extent, were the boys. Denny had become a good shot. Murdoch was good too, but more interested in fly fishing. The day of teen-age camps, or older teenagers organising their own holidays, was still far off.

At Craignish Castle, now demolished—a joint holiday with others—we played Waves in the great sunken garden where there were fine shrubs and borders, and there was a curious tripartite mini-affair involving Douglas Cole, me and a rising young Labour politician, unsatisfactory for all of us. We went swimming off Craignish Point among the seals, who clearly supposed that I, in my black rubber bathing cap, was one of them; when we landed on their stinking little island, they hardly moved to let us climb up.

Then we had a house in the Borders, where I had another unsuccessful affair. But all went to turn the mill-wheels of writing. The man in question got so cross with me at one point that he threw me across the room; I landed quite undamaged. I was equally cross because the men of the party, including Dick, had gone to see the salmon netting at the mouth of the Tweed, without me.

We had two summer holidays on Vallay. The journey from Kyle on the mainland was by a MacBrayne boat with a good deal of livestock on board and rather sick-making in a rough sea, though I wasn't worried. Over to Loch Maddy on North Uist. Then a hired car which came to a halt in the gathering dark and there was sandy machair underfoot and a torch and a boat and dark sea and a hand helping the children and me in and a voice with little English to it. Nor did the other rower have anything other than the Gaelic. All we could see in the night were a few vague small lights ahead. But in the morning Vallay Strand which we had crossed was gleaming golden sand and blue sea pools.

The house itself was not what one would call well furnished; there were great splashes of candle grease on the stairs where the owner had staggered upstairs in winter after fortifying himself against the cold. But we were out most of the time, rain or fine, and day after day we would see maybe a dozen rainbows, single or double, stretching themselves over the sea and the croft houses crouched under the weather. The sun polished the silverweed, the machair had its own wind-flattened flora and where it ended there were delicate shells brought in by the Gulf Stream and laid along the tide edges. At Griminish on the main island there was a strange little loch with a floating island of matted reed roots that one could wade out on to, carrying one's gun high—not that I shot much—and walk through the reed forest while it wobbled underfoot. On Vallay Island itself there were underground passages still unexplored, though by now they must have been measured and dated into pre-history.

Lachlan MacLean gillied for us; at least it was a little money, better than gathering whelks along the rocks. Forty years, then, have I known Lachlan MacLean, through all the next part of my life. Bella from Baleshare, down the coast a bit, cooked for us, rabbit, sea trout, lobster pie, scones, potatoes. Nurse was very much at home there, being a Gaelic speaker, and we got to know our neighbours.

There was a tiny air-strip at Sollas which gave alternative travel by five-seater planes. One summer Walter Greenwood came up with his current girlfriend, rather inappropriate there and a great consumer of time in the one bathroom.

From childhood I had been accustomed to help with any farm work and it was nothing new to me to go out and bind when the in-bye field was cut, though it was bere, nasty prickly stuff. Then the two old men who had been scytheing came and put a small straw binding round me and spoke to one another low and carefully in the Gaelic, which I did not understand. They told me to keep the binding on and go ben and I would get my wish. I realised that I was the sacrifice, the harvest queen, the *cailleach*. But I didn't get my wish, or at least not in the form which I put it into.

We could have bought Vallay Island and I at least was sorely tempted, but the house was falling to bits, the water supply doubtful, the heating by peat fires, the lighting by candles. Worse, it would have been almost impossible to grow anything in the garden without importing a shipload of soil and there was no shelter. It would have been totally impractical. All the same:

> Under the foot the soft shell crunches,
> Gabble the duck at the edge of the sand,
> The wheeling goose skein checks and bunches,
> Ah the soft air of Vallay Strand!

And anyhow, perhaps next year we might go back to lovely abroad.

However, late in 1937, the firm of Writers to the Signet in Edinburgh, which included Uncle Willie and his younger son Archie, were acting for the sellers of Carradale estate, or rather the remains of it. Most of it had gone to the Forestry Commission, while three of the tenants had bought out their land. What was left was the house and garden and the home farm with some 45 acres of arable in very poor shape and badly in need of draining and liming, all let cheap for summer grazing to neighbours, and another 250-odd acres of unprofitable rough grazing, rock, marsh, raised beach overgrown with bracken and rhododendron and various strips of woodland. But there was also a fishing river; Archie and Graeme proposed to take Mains, the farmhouse, now empty, and share the fishing. Just after Aunt Bay's funeral I went with my cousins to see the place, feeling under pressure. Sadness and resentment clouded the drive, until we stopped and ate sandwiches beyond Lochearnhead and for a little the weather cleared.

In a sense Carradale was a bargain, and everyone else wanted it. Anyhow it was only to be for holidays. My final price for agreeing was that we should employ Lachlan MacLean. There had been nothing for him in North Uist, and if he had gone to seek his fortune in Glasgow as he had half intended, I could see him selling papers on the street corner or just joining a dole queue; the depression of the Thirties was still there. He duly arrived with a wife and small son; there were a few other Gaelic speakers in Carradale, though the language was dying out.

Easter 1938 was our first family holiday at Carradale. We had done some alterations and redecoration after we took over; it was all much quicker than now and vastly cheaper. Local firms were good and careful. For the present head of the Campbeltown firm of painters, it was his first job as an apprentice and he remembers how his father told him to be extra careful in the big drawing room where the blue of walls and doors matched with the blue of Dick's great Chinese carpet. Here there was a vast marble mantelpiece; I gave it a tug and it came loose and toppled. Instead we had a long shelf above the fire and the ranges of book shelves on each side. Local joinery was excellent; I drew and had made the table where I now write—my desk was still in London.

We had put in electric light, working off our own generator, coke-fired central heating and bedroom wash-basins, only just beginning to be usual. We had not yet realised the way a strong southerly gale could blow rain right through stonework, nor the problems of disused chimney-heads and worn lead flashing. The main structural alterations were to the kitchen which was brought up to dining-room level, given a good sink, nice wide windows and an Esse stove; but even so there were steep stairs down to the storeroom, scullery and—later on when the Hydro Board electricity came—the deep-freeze. Bells were put in, though even then I thought that was stupid; only the short-circuiting mice occasionally rang them.

Most of the furniture came from Peter Jones on a 'holiday home' basis: Scandinavian-type simple design had just started and it is still acceptable, though the Finnish furniture, very fashionable at the time and not expensive, is only too well relished by wood-worm. We had not begun to think of moving up our own furniture from London. Luckily we got splendid heavy-weight curtain material from Heal's for the drawing room and library. This still survives and has got to go on doing so.

But I was still rather reluctant about the whole thing. I felt I would get into Aunt Bay's position, pulled into everything. Yet after all I was never made a J.P.; my political views forbade that in Argyll. However nobody could deny the beauty of the place and of the garden. When two of the fishermen, Denny Macintosh and Willie Galbraith, came cautiously over to see what they could get out of us, I gave them sprigs of scented lily-flowered rhododendron and also a somewhat different approach to the one they had been used to from the Tigh Mor, the big house. They went away to spread the news.

We had inherited an enormous out of door staff of which we gradually disembarrassed ourselves and were left with a garden staff of three. Not too much for the way it was then, with the walled garden hoed into weedlessness and all ivy and escallonia clipped or fastened back, the greenhouses painted and never a broken pane, the paths in the wild garden cleared and not allowed into the curves which they have amiably taken since, the long stretches of grass mowed, even the croquet lawn almost level.

There was also a splendid wire fruit cage for the soft fruit, with enormous currant bushes and row on row of raspberries. All was sustained by constant dunging and occasional cartloads of wrack when the tide brought it in. The head gardener, as in *Peter Rabbit*, was Mr MacGregor.

So it was all rather like Cloan, only more so. That summer Graeme and Archie and their party came for the fishing. Quite a number of salmon were caught. We set about improving the cottages, putting in bathrooms and damp courses, and making two good cottages out of the old dairy and outbuildings at Mains. As far as possible we had thrown open what had been strictly private estate roads and paths. The bay was now everyone's. We began to have camps including, that summer, a YCL camp from Glasgow, nice young things whose descendants, still left-wing but tending to be Labour Party, come, I'm glad to say, to camp every year for the fair fortnight.

Imperceptibly, our lives changed. I got lots of flower vases and filled them over and over again. We were all down at the harbour quite a lot; in those days there was an easy and cheap boat connection with Glasgow. Looking out of the hall window, south across Carradale Bay, there would be the *Davaar* or the *Dalriada* coming up from Campbeltown and rounding the point. Then it was time to drive down to the old pier. There were the herring boats and the fishermen. Soon enough, the boys and I were going out for a night's fishing. I began to write a long poem about it, checking up all the time on the detail. And slowly I began to know something about the ring-net herring fishing.

We quickly became involved with the village hall. It had been an idea in Carradale for some time, but there had never been any agreement on the site. However, the range of stone barns that had been part of the old Mains farm seemed almost equi-distant from the various parts of the Carradale community. Everything was settled and they held from us on a feu duty of six herrings a year from a Carradale boat—there were plenty of herrings in those days before the mid-water trawling started. John Macgregor was the architect. It was the first building of its kind: steel arches and concrete in wood shuttering, which left a pleasant surface, but somewhat upset the local builders used to smooth plaster finish. The inner walls were rough plaster combed into a wavy pattern—great fun to do. At that time there was still a great mill wheel; indeed I went on using the water-powered threshing mill for some years, until that part of the building was, later on, turned into committee rooms. Everyone was most enthusiastic and, when the war came and floor timber became unavailable, various fishermen put in for permits for wood for their boats, and turned it over to us. It was the last hall to be finished before all that was stopped.

When we got back to London that year—the year of Munich—there were more and more refugees from Hitler, people needing help, some of whom were beginning to think about Carradale as their next stop. We were all the more frightened of an immediate declaration of war because we knew how totally unprepared we were. And yet 'peace in our time' brought us little joy. What did we want, then? Denny was at Cambridge, reading medicine in his first year. How would the call-up affect him? Murdoch was still at Winchester. Would the casualties be like last time? We felt helpless.

Very soon after we came to Carradale we had started a local Labour Party branch, and after a little I realised to my embarrassment that the old tradition of doing what pleases the laird held over this too. But a few recruits were genuine and prepared to do a bit of thinking; probably there was some kind of radical feeling in the village. And in Campbeltown there was a nucleus of old miners and again a radical tradition which had made Argyll at one time a Liberal seat. We got in touch and in the fine summer of 1939 we had a Labour Party Highland Games meeting with tea and cake and piping and one of the old miners handing in his own silver cups for the competitions.

It was a full house that year, with perhaps most of us feeling that this could be the last time before whatever was coming. We joked about gas masks and shelters, but uneasily. And what was the Labour Party going to do? Elizabeth Harman was there and remembers our clever evening pencil-and-paper or general knowledge games, and how Margaret Cole always won. During the early weeks of August we went on doing the usual things, swimming, picnicking, shooting and fishing, picking flowers and fruit in the garden, thinking that perhaps somehow things might turn out differently. Well, they didn't.

I don't recollect laying in anything other than coke, for the boiler, and anthracite for the Esse stove in the kitchen. I had no deep-freeze then and anyway there did not appear to be a shortage of anything, nor did one wish to be a hoarder. A few months later, however, I was offered a considerable quantity of good quality Army stores, dirt cheap. I refused and even told the kindly offerer who had meant so well by me that he ought to know better, these things were national property, that it was unpatriotic and dishonest and goodness knows what else. They would have come in very useful!

If the hospital situation developed and River Court was taken over, it looked as if I would be stuck at Carradale. It was known that there would be an evacuation of children from all the large towns, and there would be plenty else to see to. Val, I thought, should go to the village school; I liked Mr Jackson, the headmaster, who was delighted at the idea of a pupil who would do Latin lessons with him after school. Nurse was married and away though Belle was still with us for a time. Dick had arranged to go and stay with the Coles, who had hurried back. For all of us international socialists, whatever the outcome of the war, we felt ourselves, deep inside, already defeated. Stalin and Chamberlain had seen to that.

TWO WARS IN A LIFETIME

IT SEEMED UNFAIR. Such a short time since 1918. We had put in the new stair carpet at River Court less than a year ago. The boys. *Freundschaft und Freiheit*, all for nothing. There was my brother in the *Worker*, going for the Government about the inadequacy of the Anderson shelters—but interestingly, though he was a card-carrying Communist, he was doing secret work for the Admiralty. The *Week* kept coming, with Claude Cockburn, the *New Statesman* with Kingsley Martin and others of our friends. But events were thundering over them.

By September Carradale was filling up again. I wrote for things to be sent up from London, wondering when or whether I would be seeing our house on the Mall again. One anti-Nazi refugee lady and her daughter had arrived, a young couple, the Rendels, also an old friend, Tony Pirie, with her son John, just Val's age. Her husband happened to be in America at a scientific conference. There were friends of the boys, Robin and Stewart and Hank; in fact the house was about full. We waited. At the end of August the billeting officers came round and took over Mains for the Glasgow children; I found Jean to do the cooking. There would be a teacher with them.

Mass Observation asked those on the national panel to keep a diary which I did regularly day by day:

> *September 1st.* Woke from nightmare to realise that at least it hasn't happened yet: so until after breakfast. Got the news at ten. Two of the boys had been out all night herring fishing so were asleep still; the others came in and listened. At the end Dick said 'That's torn it. . . .' Felt a bit sick. Went into the garden and saw Willie [Buchanan, the under-gardener] very white; he had been listening to Hitler 'working them up'—Willie himself conducts a choir. . . . All felt it has got to come

now. We talked of the ordinary people in Germany and tried to hope this would mean the end of privilege everywhere. Lachie was filling the car up so I waited, talking to Eddie [keeper] and Taggy [under-keeper], both of them curiously without enmity towards Germany; we discussed ploughing up the fields for potatoes and they argued as to whether they would bear two crops in succession and I said I hoped they wouldn't have to. . . . Lachie brought the car back; I said Bad news and he soberly, Aye.

Went to the kitchen to tell Bella who said 'My goodness, they'll be taking all the young men.' She began to tell me about her folk on the croft at Baleshare. Went round to the school, found Mrs Jackson and Mrs Cameron. . . . They talked about the way the billeting arrangements had broken down and of what had to be done. I offered to do anything I could; we agreed there must be central catering etc. if possible. Mrs Jackson said the church ought to take the children; they could sit there comfortably and be fed. What was the good of a church anyhow. The minister wanted his holiday; let him go over to Warsaw and see what sort of a Christian he calls himself!

Back to Mains to collect some furniture in case we have to furnish the bothy for children or others. Found Jean in tears and saying she must go home to see her parents who were in a mining district in Dumfries; calmed her down with some trouble and told her how much use she would be cooking for the children. Dick came over to try and hurry the men who were working at the new cottage as we very much want to get it finished. The question is whether they will go on with the much needed housing estate.

The two who had been out with the herring fleet were down for lunch still talking of how the *Cluaran* had got 30 shillings a basket for its fish. But mostly we talked about all this. The children were giggling rather and got on my nerves; Eglé still seemed to fear a Munich. The rest of us perhaps almost hoped for one.

. . . Met the postman who said bad weather almost automatically. Took in the letters: all the newspapers seemed sadly out of date, especially the *Worker* and the *Week*! Dick and I drove over to the school feeling more and more nightmarish. Mrs Jackson said that Jackson was away with the billeting officers, adding that they were having great difficulty.

Back to the house, heard another news, then Angus came in to measure windows for blackout. We wrote it down from room to room; . . . finished measuring and had two sheets full of measurements, looked at them hopelessly. Tea-time. Denny took the measurements and began to add them up. Seeing the tea-table with scones and new cake and jam and jelly and butter and the children and the big boys still there I began to cry. I had to keep on going out during tea-time to cry on the stairs. Dick very worried as to what he ought to do.

Six o'clock news. I simply cannot bear to hear the same things over and over. I read the papers . . . missed the first few minutes because of phoning Campbeltown to try and get dark stuff. The Co-op says you are like the rest of us, put it off till the last moment hoping it wouldn't happen, adding: we were just the same. Say they can promise nothing. Matthews however says they hope to have some in early next week and will put me on to their list.

Realise at the end of the news that there is to be a complete blackout and that only one or two rooms will be habitable. We leave Denny to paste up brown paper and drive over to school. Find Jackson and helpers with forms. Jackson says 'The very man we want!' Tells us he expects over 400 children and has only been able to billet 120. Some people have relatives or still have visitors with them. We say we will try and put up the surplus. Dick is asked to drive some of the billeting officers down to the village, which he does. One of them asks me to look in on Angus and ask him if he will take a child. I drop off at Mains and ask Annie. She says at once she will take two, not in her spare room as a relation is coming, but in the sitting room; she has been very ill and I say she must take care—they can be fed at Mains. . . . I go to Mains and talk to Jean who has, as I told her, laid in flour, cereals, prunes, sugar etc. I ask her to get a hot meal for two o'clock. Pinkie (her husband) is there, very serious, says his two young brothers are called up already in the Air Force Reserve; he doesn't want to go. We decide we can take two more children than I had thought at Mains. Angus has offered me a chair bed and his old bedstead which is in the bothy.

Back in falling dusk to look for tacks; Denny is dealing with windows etc. I find a billeting officer and tell him Angus will take two and we will take twelve more somehow. The others are having supper—the birds we shot last week. Denny still dealing with windows. I go and get the littles—my two and Tony's one—to bed; Val is rather upset and clings to me saying Will there be a war? She is afraid of her old nurse in Edinburgh being bombed. John rather upset too and clings to Tony. Find the bathroom shutters won't work after all.

The nine o'clock news. Dick looks desperately unhappy. The boys quiet and horrified. Joan cries at her husband's feet; I go over to her. The girls seem all right. Tony hopes Bill won't try and come back from America. Chamberlain's speech. Horribly like Asquith in '14. Greenwood—the die is cast! Oh, a lovely leader for our party! We take notes of the few regulations. The gladiolus on the shelf shine and ramp at us.

We go out to look at the lights, see if they are obscured in the two usable rooms. Murdoch and I unpack some things sent from London. I go to see if the girls are all right. Dick and I walk down to the sea, talking about chances and what he ought to do and about the boys and about how incredible and lunatic it is and how miserable we feel about Russia. Denny has heard earlier that he was not certainly a medical student as he hadn't done enough anatomy; the question was whether he could be specially in view of his First and scholarship. Dick talks to the other boys, urging them to stay on here till they know what to do. S[tewart] says his brother is called up and R[obin] says so must his be—but can he be got out as he speaks several foreign languages? I kiss them all and they go down to the sea. Everyone writing letters. I say I will write my diary and keep sane. . . .

September 2nd. At breakfast discussion about the children who were to come. The girls and the small children say their divans are perfectly all right without mattresses and bring the latter down, also blankets. I dissuade them from producing all their blankets with a vision of winter and unheated house. All run about fetching things. Complicated housekeeping, Bella cross! Denny in overalls painting the windows of pantry and staircase with black paint. Angus doing blinds. . . .

We listened on and off to the news but kept on bumping into idiotic dance music. I went into the garden, got apples and talked to Hugh MacGregor who was very nice. Lilla had rung up to say that she and young Dick thought the Labour Party annual meeting must be put off from tonight; I agreed. They asked after my Denny and I asked after hers. . . . We all ask after the ages of our men. . . . Talked to Hugh about ploughing up, then to the minister who was as irritating as usual. I got some sweet peas for the Mains and here, keeping Dick talking to me while I did it. All the *things* seem so extra lovely. 'Fair is the Lithe'.

Early lunch and then to pier in the car to meet the children. None by the first boat. . . .

The crew had gone out in the *Alban* last night as the fishing and the prices had been good. But Denny Mac said none of them had the heart to look for the herring; the boats were all still talking to one another across the water. The lights they knew were all out, the Cumbraes, the Skate, the Cruban and all, and it felt queer; they would have to learn again to fish without working lights as they did in the old days. Young Dick came up to us very worried, all the heart taken out of him by Russia. Colin passed, usually so gay, now miserable. Then the children's boat was sighted. Most of the village went down to see them come in. Mrs Macmillan said her husband had caught a stainlock last night and would we have it for the children. I accepted gratefully.

We made up beds with mattresses and blankets in the play-room; as it was sunny I got the mattress out of the bothy and aired it and the pillows; I took some more blankets and a lilo over. . . . Oh, yes, and more things arrived from London, including the *Encyclopaedia Britannica* and a trunkful of things the maids thought I would want. I had asked for warm things for the children; unfortunately most of what they sent was outgrown, including a marvellous assortment of outgrown bathing dresses which had somehow not been thrown away, the belt of a dress of mine—not the dress—an old hat and a few things I had wanted such as our Renaissance bronze medals, also Dick's last war medals!

We had tea and after a time Dick turned up and said that he had taken some children to Mains but there were none for us in the house. He had been taking children about to their various billets by car: said that a great many mothers in Glasgow had refused at the last minute to let their school children go and that a lot of these were mothers of pre-school children. There had been a ridiculous story started by Taggy that Hitler had disappeared and that everything was over; I told the maids it had come on the Ruritanian wireless but all the same had a funny kind of underneath feeling that it might somehow be true and one might wake up. . . . I felt that going along the terrace border picking flowers. Yet the six o'clock news was hardly disappointing; one was also prepared for evil. Eglé is obviously afraid of 'another Munich' still.

I went over to Mains to see the two teachers and four children who were there and see that everything was all right. They seemed very relieved at being in a comfortable house; Jean was terribly pleased with one of the wee girls who had started by thanking her for having her in her house and adding that her mummy had said she hoped she would come back and visit them in Glasgow. They are from Springburn, a poorish district. Many had not seen the sea even.

Denny was doing the car lights according to the new regulations and Murdoch was darkening windows. The girls went and picked blackberries; all had helped in the washing up. Jessie, my London cook, started off this morning after handing over to the hospital staff which are taking on the house, but doesn't arrive till Monday.

Of course if anything happens in Glasgow there may be a rush, but if I am to take the various London people I promised hospitality to children for and possibly the staff at the office I shall be glad not to fill up the house too much.

After dinner and the eight o'clock news we went over to see about the lighting at Mains which wants some adjusting, and talked to the teachers about future arrangements. Came back to find young Dick [Galbraith]. The fleet had come back early last night and missing the light in our house—I hated not being able to show it any longer—and prepared for any news. Young Dick had dreamt that Hitler had withdrawn and Chamberlain had flown over to do an appeasement. He wasn't sure whether he woke disappointed or relieved. He 'hates fighting but wants to have a hit at Hitler'. I asked him whether if he were a Labour premier he would immediately Poland was invaded have sent off English bombers to bomb Berlin. Denny being very anti-fascist. We discussed what was worth dying for—or killing for and all that. Between times there was a certain amount of joking and laughing of a slightly grim kind. I suppose that Lilla and I and Alec (who came round just before dinner) are the only members of the [local Labour Party] executive who just don't want a war. Not anyhow. The wireless trickled on; one felt that already muscial taste had subsided a point or two.

September 3rd. I listened to the nine o'clock news realising fairly clearly what the next was to be. The others were mostly not down but I had not slept well. Valentine went off to Mains to look after the Glasgow children; Dick and I discussed what was to be done about the education of Avrion and Valentine; the latter can go to school here for a term, but the former would learn nothing. Tony said 'I'll start this war clean' and went to wash her hair; a little later I did the same; it wasn't quite dry by 11.15. As we listened to Chamberlain speaking, sounding like a very old man, I kept on wondering what the old Kaiser was thinking, whether he was old enough to see it all as folly. The boys looked pale and worried. At the end Joan said 'How could he ask God to bless us?' Then Lois began crying and said 'The

Beast! Why couldn't he have let Germany keep Poland?' As *God Save the King* started, Denny turned it off and someone said thank you.

The maids hadn't wanted to come through; I told Annie, who was wonderfully cheerful and said she remembered the Boer War, and Bella who said 'Isn't that heartbreaking'. After a bit she began to cry, a saucepan in her hand, and said 'Think of all our men going' then to me 'Of course you've got boys too'. Dick said 'Think of the women in Germany all saying that too' but there was no response. Then she asked 'When will they send our men over?' But none of us had much idea.

In the drawing room the big boys were writing and reading; I think perhaps writing poetry. I was feeling sick and so was S. H[ank] and I went over to Mains but the teachers had just left. Valentine had brought the Glasgow children over; they were talking happily, but looked very white and thin and small. The village was empty; most people at church. It began to rain hard and we took shelter at the Galbraiths'. Young Dick said 'So it's come'. Then he began asking H.: 'What are you going to do?' He seemed less enthusiastic than he'd been the night before when he thought 'appeasement' was possible, said he didn't think he'd ever be able to shoot anyone and he would rather do minesweeping. H. explained his position, that he wouldn't fight but might do work of national importance—he was too much attached to things and people to be able to be a clear pacifist.* They talked about the possibility of dropping leaflets instead of bombs on German towns and then we talked about these words people used—national honour and justice and all that. Dick said Russia was going to be neutral; we kept on thinking how little there had been on the wireless about Russia.

We looked in at Mains and found the children very cheerfully having dinner, but the teachers were worried because some of the mothers were saying it was so quiet and lonely that

* As things turned out Hank went into the Navy and was killed a year later. He was the first of the young ones to go.

they couldn't stand it and were going back if they paid their own fares.

At lunch Joan said she was on a small island of sand with everything cut off before and behind. I said I had been feeling the future cut off for some time. We all agreed it was queer to feel the past so cut off, everything had a different meaning now. The two o'clock news and Greenwood's speech which somehow made the official Labour people feel rather sick.

From then until four-thirty I went round with Miss Simpson, the teacher, the superintendent, a very nice and efficient Miss Knight, and James MacKinven, who was one of the billeting officers. I told them not to worry because one child had swallowed a prune stone; they said what about a doctor; I explained that our doctor was only just back from an appendicitis, we had no district nurse though we had been hoping to get one, but the doctor's wife was a nurse and I had trained during the last war.

At Portrigh we found one lot of boys all right, but next door two little girls, nine and eleven, who had cried solidly since they came; we said we would take them at Mains. We had already got another two who hadn't been happy in their billets. We found one woman with four children of her own who was a bit stuck in a very nice little house without provisions, as she had not been able to buy them on Saturday evening and no one had realised she would need them. I said I would provide them and get hold of some other things she needed. I rather acted as 'lady of the manor' but I had to. I said I would get a shed cleared out and we would start a play centre and asked if I could do some teaching.

We took the two crying girls back; I told them stories and they brightened up, but a tremendous thunderstorm began; we ran and they clung on to me. Before we were at Mains I was wet through in spite of my mac. The thunder was crashing overhead with almost continuous lightning and the rain so thick it was hard to breathe; when I got in the helper was rather hysterical and Jean a bit frightened. Pinky, dead sober now, had been very helpful. The lightning pinged and zipped and broke a couple of electric bulbs; it all seemed very appropriate. . . . I got back to the house, changed and dried my hair, and the boys talked, taking in this gulf we have stepped over. R. said 'all my tastes are pre-war!' And they all began saying things were pre-war; there was a certain amount of genuine laughter. . . . Denny went on with his Anatomy.

The Mains children had been having a grand time dressing up and were very cheerful. After tea we had the six o'clock news; three of the maids came for the King's speech. . . .

The storm had broken a lot of the beautiful gladiolus and brought down some apples; at least it is a natural thing.

Young Dick came over, a bit worried about what he should do; we all advise him to stay where he is in the fishing fleet. . . .

One feels curiously out of it here; in fact there is no war yet here, only marvellous moonlight over the trees. It is odd not having heard yet from anyone in London about coming up with children. We all kept on noticing how these last two days have been a parody of all the Auden, Isherwood stuff; we might have been 'on the frontier'. I suppose the announcers just can't help parodying themselves.

September 4th. Tony woke, saying it was the third morning, but would one go on feeling like this the three-hundreth. I heard the end of Roosevelt and the nine o'clock news; no one else was down. At breakfast we were thinking about education, trying to assemble our knowledge; all the boys knew things accurately, so did Tony and Jim, on their own subjects. My knowledge is perhaps wider than anyone's, but astonishingly inaccurate. When I went to the kitchen Bella told me about the *Athena*, making it out worse than it was; several people told me she had sailed from Glasgow, also that there were three Carradale men in the crew—I have not been able to verify this, but I should be surprised if it was any truer than the Glasgow sailing. I went into the room and said that a liner had been torpedoed; Tony burst into tears before I had time to tell her it was not one *from* New York—Bill no doubt is still in that dangerous city where one is so apt to be run over in the street.

We made various plans for winter and early spring vegetables, Tony making suggestions about vitamins. Hugh MacGregor is full of ideas about keeping hens and growing barley and oats for them—of course this means a two-year plan but I suppose one must attempt that. I left Jim to discuss hens with him. I feel very reluctant to interfere too much with the flowers; we are already growing more vegetables than before. We can't do much this winter, but we shall try and keep up some green-stuff. . . . Then I picked flowers and made a list of necessary drugs for the school authorities to order. I think it has been taken and ordered quite uncritically!

From two to nearly seven I drove Miss Knight, the superintendent of the Springfield school, Mr Jackson and one or two teachers. We went over to see what was happening to people in the outlying districts. We stopped at Grogport, Crossaig, etc. and talked to mothers and children, the former all rather fed up. At Skipness we found a teacher with several children in a rather messy house; she had found bugs and cooking was extremely difficult; no one had helped them except the local teachers. The obvious thing was to get them into Carradale. . . . We completely lost one teacher, but at last found her at the big house at Crossaig, very happy. But one mother and children left from near Skipness, another we saw said 'It's very quiet', but it became harder and harder as the day went on to believe in a real war.

When I got back I found a rumour that the *Bremen* had been captured.

The Glasgow children had gone round to the pier with the fleet, Denny Mac being particularly nice to them. Our boys had been cleaning out the old garage for a play centre and had discovered a fine Victorian fire engine. Lois said that the Glasgow children she had been talking to hated the food here. . . . We talked about poetry; I typed Dick's Elland article. We didn't listen in at eleven.

And so it went on, with organisation and people and the refugee children from Glasgow gradually drifting back. We were tensed up for something which was not happening, at least not to us in Great Britain.

But as the phoney war hotted up I got more anxious and no less involved with the possible farming operations, the village, and especially the building of the village hall. Eddie and Taggy were called up, but Lachlan stayed to help me, though his farm experience had been in the Outer Hebrides, almost as different as mine in the Thames valley.

Val was by now at Carradale School, probably playing up the teachers to near breaking point. John Pirie was there for a couple of terms, also Phina, the daughter of an ex-secretary of mine, who because the war was not turning out to be the revolutionary success that her anarchist group had planned for with themselves leading it, really took it out on me. People came and went, sometimes rather demandingly. Rationing was brought in. The garden was still full of glorious flowers but Hugh MacGregor was a somewhat fierce and sombre, probably frustrated, character who clearly felt himself capable of running everything better than I did. He wanted everything up so as to plant potatoes, not warning me about how necessary the shelter hedges were. Bella developed the habit of leaving her false teeth in a saucer on the kitchen table covered by a pudding basin which one was liable to lift off and almost get bitten. There were more and more forms to fill in. more decisions which I had to make personally while I was at Carradale and Dick in London staying with the Coles and worrying because he was considered too old for most of the things he wanted to do.

In May 1940 the war suddenly became serious, desperately serious. Some of my friends' children, including John Pirie, had been sent over to the United States or Canada, especially if they had relations there. I had many offers and was increasingly worried about Avrion at school in the south. But both he and Valentine were determined not to leave the country. When the Mass Observation national panel was asked in the summer of 1940 if they expected an invasion I answered yes. We were screwing ourselves up.

Meanwhile Denny was in trouble at Cambridge for being found

with a WOMAN in his rooms. The woman, Ruth, very sensibly said that they were engaged to be married and got off rather more lightly than Denny, who was sent down, but they were both well on their way to being qualified as doctors. The Piries were a splendid standby for Ruth who was the best medical student of her year. They came up after term and it made all the difference to me having Ruth there and a wedding in the air, some tangible bit of the future to hold on to. I had been so happy to be pregnant again; that too was the future. But what was it going to be?

With one bit of myself I was going on planning on something like the existing basis but on the other hand I was considering the possibility of the house being taken over by the Gauleiter of Kintyre and what then? It was happening in other countries. Why not here? In the event of invasion where was my loyalty? Should I at risk of my life, as seemed in many ways preferable, do everything to destroy the Germans (such as putting cyanide into the wine—but would that have been noticeable?) but risk their revenge not only on Carradale but also on the evacuated children for whom I was responsible? Or should I at least pretend to collaborate? This was made a somewhat easier choice when I found I was in Hitler's Black Book—it was then, I remember, and in a sudden panic, that I asked one of the fishermen if he could get me and any of the children who were there across to Canada in a fishing boat. He of course said 'Och aye, easy' at which I realised how stupid I was being.

I had intended to have my confinement in Glasgow though Aunt Edith had kindly offered to take me in at Cloan. But that seemed increasingly pointless and the specialist—I'd had some difficulties during the pregnancy—offered to come over to Carradale.

By mid-June most of the evacuees were back in Glasgow, but we had been told unofficially that there might be a re-evacution. We hoped we might get different ones! I was getting increasingly into farming with Lachlan, whose English was much improved though he went on swearing in Gaelic, helping me. And the local farmers lent me gear and advised me.

The land here was in such a bad state that I couldn't even get a cutting of meadow hay off it. I had to start the hard way. We got a light horse who worked in a pair with one of the garrons. During the next years I harrowed and mowed with them. I worked summer and winter, spreading dung with a dung fork, sowing oats or grass seed equally by hand, crawling on the ground singling turnips, snedding in the December cold. Because of all this and because it is now decent farm land, I feel it is mine in a way that is far from unreal legalities.

And meanwhile in and around Kintyre, war preparations went on, road blocks planned and the blowing up of bridges. Signposts were taken down and even place names from buses or carts. The news got worse and worse. Narvik. The old place names from World War I began to come back. Sedan. Dunkirk. Saint Valéry. Paris. In mid-June my diary says 'What will happen to us all in another fortnight?' At the beginning of July the specialist duly came over and everything went ahead. But my baby died.

INDEX OF NAMES

Persons, places and organizations dealt with in some detail in the text

NM = Naomi Mitchison